THE FRAGMENT-ING OF ADVENTISM

THE FRAGMENT- ING OF ADVENTISM

Ten Issues Threatening the Church Today
Why the Next Five Years are Crucial

WILLIAM G. JOHNSSON

Pacific Press Publishing Association
Boise, Idaho
Oshawa, Ontario, Canada

Edited by Kenneth R. Wade
Designed by Tim Larson and Mark Winchester
Cover photo by Nona Guerriere
Typeset in New Century Schoolbook 11/13

Unless otherwise noted, all Scripture quotations are taken
from the New International Version.

Library of Congress Cataloging-in-Publication Data:

Johnsson, William G., 1934-
    The fragmenting of Adventism : ten issues threaten-
ing the church today : why the next five years are
crucial / William G. Johnsson.
        p. cm.
    1. Seventh-day Adventists—Doctrines. 2. Seventh-
day Adventists—Membership.   I. Title.
BX6154.J65 1995
286.7'32—dc20   94-48406
                                                  CIP

95 96 97 98 99 • 5 4 3 2 1

Contents

Preface

About ten years ago I began to sense that something new was happening in the Seventh-day Adventist Church, particularly in North America. It went beyond FDR—Ford, Davenport, and Rea—the triple blows that hammered the church in quick succession at the beginning of the 1980s. Something was moving; a new breeze was stirring.

The decade of the eighties was the most turbulent and difficult in my experience. During the first half, the church was wracked by forces that seemed ready to tear it apart. For many, the "in" thing was to put down the church, its standards, its leaders, Ellen White. It was as though the spirit of the 1960s that convulsed American society had sprung up twenty years later among Seventh-day Adventists.

At the *Adventist Review*, we were in the eye of the storm. I joined the staff as an associate editor immediately following the 1980 Glacier View meeting that examined and rejected the views of the popular teacher and preacher Desmond Ford. I assumed the editor's chair on December 1, 1982, just when the crisis precipitated by the collapse of the Davenport financial scheme was bursting out all over. During those years, many Adventists, feeling disillusioned, frustrated, or just plain angry, vented their passion on the

7

Review. We got many long, harsh letters. Not a few members, regardless of how they felt about the *Review* itself, expressed their anger by canceling their subscriptions.

I spent a lot of time on the road during those years. My study and writing on the book of Hebrews put me in the forefront of the theological debate, and I was asked to speak at many workers' meetings and other church gath erings. I always allowed plenty of time for questions and answers, and sometimes the sessions would drag on for hours. A typical weekend started with a Friday-evening vespers, took in the Sabbath-morning preaching service, and gave over the rest of the Sabbath to frank and some-times heated, bitter questioning. I would return home utterly drained: it wasn't easy having people's generalized rage focused on me simply because I came from the General Conference.

Well, the anger slowly subsided. Many ministers and members, weary of argument, tuned out theological dis-cussion. And, of course, many no longer were with us— they had dropped out.

Then, as the nineties drew near, I began to sense that the halcyon days were gone. We had entered a new era, one far less predictable, more fraught with dangers for the church, but perhaps holding bright hopes also. The church would never return to the relative calm, ordered patterns of the 1960s and 1970s.

Anciently, the men of Issachar "understood the times" (1 Chronicles 12:32). Since the mid-1980s, I have tried especially to do just that—understand the times—and to help others understand them also.

The world is moving fast, and so is the church. Our situation in the mid-1990s differs vastly from that of the mid-1980s. We face new and barely articulated dangers, and I believe the next five years will be crucial for Seventh-day Adventists. But the Lord is also opening new and barely glimpsed possibilities before our eyes.

This manuscript had its origins in a talk I gave at Avondale College early in 1994. Invited to Australia to give a series of lectures to a group of church elders gathered from around that country and New Zealand, I decided at short notice to take up the topic of this book. The effect on the group was electric and shaped the whole week we were together. Two months later I presented the same material, expanded somewhat, to a meeting of Adventist editors and communicators in Seattle. Russ Holt, vice-president for editorial at Pacific Press Publishing Association, was present and heard the paper; he approached me immediately and asked me to develop it into book form.

These are my views about the future shape of the church; they have no official standing. They are based on facts, but inevitably they are speculative.

The breeze I felt years ago is still blowing. It has become a gale. Where will it take us? What lies ahead?

I'm very concerned about what will happen in the next five years. But I'm optimistic also. This book will tell you why.

One

Miracle Church

A paraphrase of Charles Dickens's famous line seems appropriate for the Seventh-day Adventist Church today—it is the best of times; it is the worst of times.

The church has entered a stage of unparalleled growth and influence. As I write, membership, according to the rolls, is lapping the eight million mark, but many more people than these consider themselves Adventists. When census takers ask the populace to indicate their religion in countries like Kenya, for instance, the government figures greatly exceed the church's. Add to these the large numbers of secret believers in Moslem lands and elsewhere, and worldwide, probably about twenty million people consider themselves Seventh-day Adventists.

Day by day the rate of accessions increases. Every forty-eight seconds someone joins the church; every five hours a new church is organized.

But the Adventist Church means more than statistics. These numbers—each one of them—have names. They stand for people, real people, wonderful people. And, worldwide, most of these people are young, in their teens and twenties.

Several years ago I spent four weeks visiting with our believers in South America. Their youth, their sheer en-

11

ergy and enthusiasm overwhelmed me. Everywhere I went, I met crowds of eager, clear-eyed, good-looking young people.

The church there self-confidently proclaims the everlasting gospel from the rooftops. Adventists capitalize on the religious calendar—especially Christmas and Easter—to connect with spiritual interest. By means of advertising, mass literature distribution geared to the season, huge posters, parades, and drama, they take the message of Jesus to the streets. And young people are at the forefront of this happy, colorful, energetic endeavor.

On a Sabbath morning, I stepped into an Adventist church in Manaus, on the Amazon in upper Brazil. Sabbath School was in progress, and the church was filled with people studying the Word together in small classes. I looked around at the teachers and then at the students: in the whole church I could find only a few people with gray hair.

I chose a class taught by a young woman. She greeted me in Portuguese and continued to teach. Her manner was lively, animated, and although I could not understand what she was saying, I could tell she had the attention of everyone in the class and was doing a superb job.

As I watched and admired, a question kept running through my head: *How old are you, young lady?* She looked quite young, but years ago I gave up trying to figure people's ages, especially women's.

At the close of the class, I was able to meet the teacher. Through an interpreter, I asked: "What is your name?"

"Maria."

"And how old are you, Maria?"

"Sixteen."

"How long have you taught in Sabbath School?"

"Two years."

Maria epitomizes Adventists in South America—young

people enthusiastically, joyfully, confidently living and sharing their religion with other young people.

But "Maria" can be found in many other parts of the world also. What is happening in South America is replicated in Inter-America, across the vast continent of Africa, and in countries of the Pacific Rim. The global Seventh-day Adventist Church, young and dynamic, is booming.

Each year the everlasting gospel reaches farther and farther, bursting the barriers of unentered areas, claiming disciples for Jesus at earth's remotest bounds. The Global Mission thrust of recent years has brought enormous interest and incentive to attempt to do the impossible. Adventists are taking seriously their marching orders from Jesus, the Lord of the mission: "Jesus came and said to them, 'All authority in heaven and on earth has been given to me. Go therefore and make disciples of all nations, baptizing them in the name of the Father and of the Son and of the Holy Spirit, teaching them to observe all that I have commanded you; and lo, I am with you always, to the close of the age' " (Matthew 28:18-20, NRSV).

We are a people of a dream. We dream dreams and see visions. Old people see them. And especially young ones.

For more than a century, a divine prophecy has motivated us, compelling and impelling us into all the world. That prophecy takes the great commission and puts it in a last-days setting: "Then I saw another angel flying in midair, and he had the eternal gospel to proclaim to those who live on the earth—to every nation, tribe, language and people. He said in a loud voice, 'Fear God and give him glory, because the hour of his judgment has come. Worship him who made the heavens, the earth, the sea and the springs of water' " (Revelation 14:6, 7).

So Adventists go into all the world. They take the good news of a crucified, risen, and soon-coming Saviour. They dream the impossible dream and give their lives to make it happen.

I have seen them across the face of the earth. I have seen them risking their lives in war-torn societies. I have seen them laboring cheerfully on in desperately isolated places, far from home and from the mail. I have seen them in Cambodia, I have seen them in Albania, I have seen them in India, I have seen them in Vietnam. From the Mekong to the Amazon, from the Yellow River to the Black Sea, from Timbuktu to Tbilis, and from Beijing to Bombay they are spreading the word, making a difference—young and old, professionals and nonprofessionals, preachers and laity. They have caught a vision; they follow the impossible dream.

But, you may counter, this is all well and good, but what about North America? Your examples all come from somewhere else.

True—the church in North America currently is not part of the extremely rapid expansion. But signs of vitality abound here, also, if we will open our eyes. One of the most positive indicators is the upsurge in volunteer service in recent years. Huge numbers of Adventists—far more than ever in our history—give a week, two weeks, four weeks, even several months or a year to build schools and churches, to provide needy people with clean water, or to teach. And in addition to all these are the scores of pastors and evangelists who go abroad to conduct evangelistic campaigns in countries where the harvest is ripe but the workers are few.

No question about it—for the Seventh-day Adventist Church, it is the best of times. Our message was never more relevant or embraced by so many. Adventists have spread into more than two hundred countries, and within each country, each year, the extent of penetration reaches deeper.

And that's not all! In a manner unprecedented, Adventists are impacting public life.

An Adventist asked to sing at the national convention of the Democratic Party? An Adventist invited to the White House to sing for the presidential prayer breakfast? An Adventist requested to sing for Billy Graham's Moscow series? An Adventist personally acquainted with Oprah Winfrey, Diana Ross, and other stars of the media?

Yes, yes, yes, and yes! Not just an Adventist, but an Adventist minister, unashamed of his profession, pastor of a large and rapidly growing congregation just a few blocks from the U.S. Capitol.

Wintley Phipps.

Who could have dreamed of such a day?

Elder Phipps is undoubtedly the best-known Adventist in public life in North America, but he is by no means alone. One of the world's great conductors, the acclaimed maestro of the San Francisco Symphony Orchestra, likewise is a Seventh-day Adventist. Herbert Blomstedt's contracts— and he is booked up to nine years ahead—state that he will lead no rehearsals during Sabbath hours. When you are in a class by yourself, you can dictate the terms!

More and more Adventists are rising to great prominence. The Lord promised Israel of old that if they would follow His ways, He would make them the head and not the tail (see Deuteronomy 28:13), and He is doing just that for His people today. His word never fails!

Look at what is happening at Loma Linda University. The infant heart transplant program leads the world, giving life to children doomed to an early death, restoring hope to despairing parents. The national media have picked up the story and produced glowing documentaries of emotive power and incalculable value to the good name of the university.

And that's not all! The proton-beam accelerator, first of

its kind in a medical setting anywhere—yes, that's *anywhere* in the world—is setting the pace in cancer treatment and attracting widespread interest.

Overseas, the public impact of Adventists is even more marked than in North America. When the new leaders of Uganda, trying to bring together that beautiful nation ravaged by Idi Amin's regime and the subsequent fighting, sought for a person of integrity to be the first prime minister, they turned to a devoted Seventh-day Adventist physician, Dr. Samson Kisekka. And in other countries of Africa as well as in the newly emerged nations of the South Pacific, you will find many Adventists serving not only as members of parliament but as cabinet ministers and heads of government departments.

And that's not all! The Adventist lifestyle, for so long considered so peculiar—no tobacco, no alcohol, vegetarian diet, exercise—has come in for massive praise from modern scientific studies. It works—that's the bottom line. Adventists live longer: on average, 8.9 years if you are male, 7.5 years if you are female.

Listen, mark my word as I wrap around me the prophet's mantle for a moment. It has not happened yet, but the day will come when a Seventh-day Adventist will be awarded a Nobel Prize!

It's inevitable. God is in this movement, so there's no stopping it. And no stopping gifted individuals who put Him first. In every field of human endeavor, Adventists are rising to the top like the cream, and more and more will rise, and the world will stand back in amazement.

All this is of the Lord's doing, I believe. His work will not finish in a corner; it will not be some little bunch of people out in the sticks who complete it. No! His everlasting gospel *flies* in midheaven, for all the world to see; He proclaims it in a *loud* voice so no one from earth's last hour can fail to hear it.

To a doubting, jaded, skeptical world in the end time, He says: "Look at them! They are *My* people! Cast in your lot with them!"

Now, lest someone take from my words a wrong impression, let me state how I regard the Seventh-day Adventist Church in relation to other faith communions. I do *not* believe that we alone are God's people. I do *not* believe that we are without fault. I do *not* believe that God is working only through us. God has His people everywhere—His true followers—and He knows who they are. Nor is God's Spirit bound or limited. God is sovereign, free, and works where and through whom He chooses.

But I believe that there is a "specialness" about the Seventh-day Adventist Church. I believe that we are the people of the remnant message described in Revelation 12:17. I believe that to us the Lord has entrusted an end-time message, even that of Revelation 14.

And because He has, and because many Adventists have taken Him seriously, good things are happening in the Seventh-day Adventist Church. With very little effort, I could gather together stories and information from around the globe and compile a new book of Acts, one every bit as wonderful, every bit as exciting. Beyond a doubt, it is the best of times for the Seventh-day Adventist Church.

But it is also the worst of times, and that is what the rest of this book will take up. We face pressures and factors today that would rip us apart as never before in our history. We face the possibility of schism more than any time since the Kellogg crisis ninety years ago.

And these pressures—pressures of fragmentation—will continue to increase. Each year that dawns will more insistently call the miracle into question: Can the church continue united?

This question is crucial because the Seventh-day Adventist Church is a miracle church beyond all that we

17

have described in this chapter—beyond the amazing growth, beyond the prominence of individual Adventists in our times. The church, *in itself*, is a miracle.

Among the hundreds of Protestant denominations, you will not find another like ours. Whereas all others, if they exist worldwide, are a loose confederation of national churches, ours is one universal faith communion—one in beliefs, mission, way of life, structure, and hope. There is nothing else like this out there—nothing even remotely like it.

If you are a Lutheran in North America, for example, you primarily find your sense of identity as a member of a particular Lutheran synod. You may have little to do with Lutherans in North America who belong to a different brand of Lutheranism—in fact, you may not be on speaking terms with some of them. And you have little sense of fellowship or solidarity with Lutherans in Germany, Asia, or elsewhere.

All other—*all* other—Protestant churches are essentially *national* churches. Adventists are unique: we are a *world* church, not a confederation of national churches.

The only other body that comes close to the miracle of the Seventh-day Adventist Church is the Roman Catholic communion. They are a huge body, and like us they are worldwide; but they also are fractured doctrinally and in practice along regional and national lines.

We face the threat of fracturing also—that's what this book is about. Can the miracle continue—the miracle of one global church?

We will look at factors that would fragment the church in the following chapters. I don't claim to be exhaustive, but I see ten areas that cause me concern. Some of these factors are new, some are old; some are old ones that have returned in a new setting or with a new intensity. Some have simply come upon us, but others are directly of our making. Some are theological, and some are not.

The order in which I deal with these factors does not indicate my sense of the relative importance of each—the first one isn't necessarily the most critical, for instance. Nor does the amount of space I devote to each suggest priorities. I simply have not attempted to assign order: only the Lord knows which are the most important. He no doubt also knows of others I haven't thought of.

What would be *your* list? Which ten factors do you see pushing our church toward fragmentation? Take a moment and jot down your ideas.

Now, here is my list.

CHAPTER
Two

The Spirit of the Age

I n the early 1930s, a Scandinavian writer, Aksel Sandemose, wrote a book about a sailor who went ashore to seek a new and different life. This man had a problem: he was terribly unsure of himself and suffered from a low self-image. Why? He had come from a place called Jante, where he had been ruthlessly put down lest he think too highly of himself.

From these origins has arisen what the Scandinavians now call "Jante-law." It is a menacing attitude that projects itself as: "Don't think that you are somebody. You are no better than the rest of us! You are no wiser, and you don't know any more than us, nor can you do anything that the rest of us can't do. Just don't think you have anything to teach us."[*]

No doubt the socialistic mind-set of the Scandinavian countries and of much of Europe provides fertile soil for Jante-law. Under the rubric of equalizing all individuals, society puts a restrictive check or control on anyone who would rise above the masses—whether through election, appointment, achievement, or natural gifts. Here the *common* person is made the measure of all things, so no one must be other than common.

Those who rise to the top find their position very uncomfortable in such an environment. The populace feels a need to control them, to remind them that they aren't somebody special. "You are what you are because we have made you what you are," is the attitude. "And remember—we can just as quickly unmake you!"

Although Jante-law hasn't reached the same level in North America, evidence of its presence abounds. Our society, which, on the one hand, glorifies celebrities—look at magazines like *People* and *Us* and the cult of personality in the media—on the other, excels in cutting down celebrities.

So throughout the 1992 presidential election campaign, the media flocked to a new young face—Bill Clinton's. He was their Prince Charming; George Bush was boring. Hillary Clinton was intelligent and svelte, the new American woman; Barbara Bush, although respected by the masses, was dismissed as grandmotherly and domestic, a relic of the old ways.

But behold the turning of the tables! Clinton had hardly finished basking in the glow of his inaugural triumph, and Hillary was still experimenting with her hairdo, when the onslaught began. The media have savaged the presidential couple ever since, pouncing on weighty matters like their tax write-off for gifts of used underwear. Intent on finding a scandal in their Whitewater investment, they are out to show that Bill is not so great after all, nor is Hillary so smart.

Jante-law with a vengeance!

Celebrities, beware! Though you go from rags to riches, from obscurity to instant recognition, your fall will come just as fast. And the media that catapulted you to stardom will relish just as garishly your public demise.

No one—but *no one*—is secure from this instant reversal. A Michael Jackson suddenly finds his career in ruins, his long-term sponsors abandoning him like rats fleeing a sinking ship, because a boy comes out of nowhere and accuses him of molestation. No proof, no police charges, but the tabloids and the talk shows placard the story, and Michael is toppled.

The stance of the media is: There just *have* to be skeletons in everyone's closets, so keep on rooting around till you find them. Investigative reporting too often means digging for dirt rather than searching for the truth.

In the United States, Jante-law has taken a typically American twist. We have invented and raised to great power someone totally outside the action—the analyst. In sports broadcasts the analyst doesn't call the plays but second-guesses them; shielded from the pressures of snap decisions and human interaction, he sits in the broadcast booth pontificating on what play might or should have been called. The analyst is always right, and the viewer identifies with him. But this is just another way of applying Jante-law and cutting down the coach to size.

Jante-law makes leadership terribly difficult in these times. This is the age of the anti-hero and the anti-leader. Because of modern means of communication and the all-pervasive analyst, the public can quickly identify the issues. They expect immediate solutions—and there's the rub. Some problems defy solution because they involve the tangled web of human relations, our prejudices, history, fears, envy, and greed. Look at the mess in the former Yugoslavia, in Haiti, in Somalia. To identify the problem in no way helps one to suggest a solution.

Inevitably, since the church is in the world, Jante-law invades the church also. Jante-law challenges and rejects authority, delights in pointing out leaders' failures, and wears them out with a steady drumbeat of negativism. Thus, it tends to weaken and fragment the church by opposing strong, centralized leadership.

Two other aspects of the spirit of the age—individualism and the confusion of style with substance—add to the pressures toward fragmentation of the church.

The cover of the *Atlantic Monthly* for February 1994 portrayed a collapsing globe. That's our world: all around we see the collapse of values, mores, and institutions. Pressure groups, rebellion, demands—the age of tribalism is upon us.

Rampant individualism leads to pluralism, and pluralism to relativism. *My* pleasures, *my* likes and dislikes, *my* gratification rule the day. Forget about the future—the children and the grandchildren—forget about who will pay later, forget about rules, and forget about God. *Don't get in my way!* If it feels good to me, I want it, and I want it now, and I'm gonna get it.

Because of raging individualism, the United States, and indeed, most societies have become almost ungovernable. So many voices calling for attention, so many factions demanding a piece of the pie. And back of it all lies the crass greed of the individual, wanting more and trying to avoid paying, putting self above the common good.

The zeitgeist—the spirit of the age—runs directly counter to what God wants to accomplish through the church. The spirit of the age fractures the church, breaking it up into groups separated and divided along caste, color, gender, and social lines; God wants to bring together all people under the banner of the everlasting gospel. The spirit of the age smashes the world church into discrete congregations that live and die to themselves, hoarding their resources to themselves and heaping them upon themselves; God wants to prepare one universal body.

Added to all the above is the confusion of style with substance.

The 1960 presidential debates between John F. Kennedy and Richard M. Nixon marked a watershed, not only in United States politics, but in society at large.

Here was a widely known public figure, vice-president of

the United States for eight years, a world traveler who had debated and matched wits with Nikita Kruschev on international television. Supremely confident of his abilities—eight years before, his "Checkers" speech at the dawn of the television age had rescued for him the Republican party's vice-presidential nomination—Nixon shrugged off the advice of Dwight D. Eisenhower and other party advisers not to give the little-known senator from Massachusetts the free publicity of national television. Nor did Nixon bother to prepare: he campaigned to the last and disdained the use of makeup before he went on camera.

And the results were disastrous for him. Viewers saw him as gaunt, haggard; without makeup, his skin looked sickly and unshaven. Meanwhile, Kennedy, rested and bronzed, came across as relaxed, healthy, and vigorous.

Those debates put Kennedy in the White House. But they did more: for the first time in American public life they ensured that style would command at least an equal place alongside substance. How a person *looked* would be as important as what he or she had to offer.

Under the influence of television viewing, that trend has gone much farther. No longer do style and substance compete as equals: style has superseded substance. No longer what a person says, no longer the quality of his ideas—the impression he leaves on the viewer is all in all.

It's enlightening to compare and contrast the reactions of radio and television audiences to national debates. They often will be vastly different. What if people had only the cold, hard words in print, as most Americans had for the Lincoln-Douglas debates? Or what if those debates had taken place one hundred years later—would Douglas rather than Lincoln have become president? Old Abe may have been the most honest candidate around, but how many people today, seeing that unhandsome exterior, would vote for him?

Those 1960 debates changed forever the way Americans understand reality; did they change the Seventh-day Adventist Church also? Is our church better or worse because of the age of television?

I stand behind progress and modern technology. I want my church to utilize every new invention, every new agent of communication for the spread of the everlasting gospel. So I am glad for the opportunities that television offers. Think of Net 95—the linking of churches throughout North America by satellite for public evangelism. Think of how the color and excitement of a General Conference session can be brought into living rooms of millions of Adventists around the world.

But I have to raise these questions of television: Has TV fostered confusion among both church leaders and members over style and substance? Has it tended to make us more shallow, tied to appearances? Has it promoted the spirit of instant analysis, instant issues, and the demand for instant solutions? And above all, since television in its essence is a one-on-one medium, has it encouraged individualism at the expense of community?

To the extent that the answer is Yes to any or all of these questions, the onset of television has helped to fragment the church.

What I am saying is that the very spirit of the times in which we live would rip the church apart. Everywhere, on all sides, society is breaking up, and the spirit that is causing society to disintegrate infiltrates the church and would smash us also.

True, at times in the past, the church has come across as rigid and authoritarian. So have some leaders. In some parts of the world—a very few, I expect—the power game may still be played out.

But today, especially in the West, the situation has reversed itself.

If once church leadership drew up plans and programs and imposed them from top down, now any idea originating with the top faces the likelihood of instant rejection, regardless of merit.

If once leaders took too much authority upon themselves, forgetting that in biblical terms *all* the people of God, both church employees and nonemployees, are the laity, today, they face massive challenges to the concept of authority itself.

If once the clergy controlled elections and committees, giving the "laity" only token representation, today, laity demand accountability (good in itself) and reduction of structures (may or may not be for the best).

If once workers' meetings put guilt trips on pastors, today, many conference presidents can't even get their workers to attend.

If once congregations followed the will of the conference unquestioningly, today, some go their own way, disregarding church policies, even in the handling of church funds.

It's a terrible time to try to lead the United States. It's a terrible time to try to lead a city, a college, a university. It's a terrible time to try to lead anything.

You can expect to be bounced from adulation to humiliation, built up and cut down, admired and vilified. You'll be quoted and misquoted, damned for what you do and what you don't do, for what you say and what you don't say. There will be plenty of people who think they're just as smart or smarter than you are, who will second-guess and tell you how stupid or yellow-livered you are. It won't be enough to *do* what is right—how people perceive you will mean more to them, so you can do the right thing and still be damned in the people's judgment.

It's a terrible time to lead the church. Yes, the Seventh-day Adventist Church. As wonderful as this fellowship is— I haven't backed away one inch from my remarks in the previous chapter—the spirit of the age, infiltrating the church, would make leadership well-nigh impossible.

A case in point: one independent-minded, charismatic character by the name of John Osborne of Florida. For a few years, Osborne worked as a minister of the Seventh-day Adventist Church, although he was never ordained as a pastor. Soon he quit church employ and started his own ministry, centering in a televised outreach. Relations with the organized church steadily deteriorated, and after a process of discussion and counsel, the Florida Conference executive committee disfellowshiped him (his membership was with the conference, not a local church).

File closed on John Osborne? In an earlier generation, it would have been, but not in these times. A small Seventh-day Adventist church in Troy, Montana, accepted him into membership—although he still lived and worked in Florida.

What happened to the concept of the congregation? What happened to the sense of solidarity of congregations?

But the story didn't end there. After the Troy church refused to heed the counsel of the Montana Conference in this matter, the conference leaders called a constituency meeting to take up the actions of the Troy church. That meeting ended, sadly, in the delegates voting to disband the Troy church.

So once again Osborne had no membership in the Seventh-day Adventist Church. But not for long: soon a church in California invited him to join them!

Whatever is happening? Understand, now, why it's such a terrible time to try to lead, even in our church?

The zeitgeist—a spirit that's anti-authority, anti-leaders, obsessively individualistic, that sets up celebrities and waits to topple them, that plays up the superficial over the solid—tends with every accelerating force to fragment the church.

The spirit of the age is so strong that it will sweep us away if we do nothing. It will plunge us into division and congregationalism. It will rip apart the church as one body. It will destroy our worldwide, unified fellowship. It will make the work of leaders impossible.

We need to be aware of the times and the spirit of the times. We need discernment to take what is good and to reject what is bad. We need heavenly eyesalve as never before.

But as powerful as the spirit of the age may be, our God is more powerful. "You, dear children, are from God and have overcome them, because the one who is in you is greater than the one who is in the world. They are from the world and therefore speak from the viewpoint of the world, and the world listens to them. We are from God, and whoever knows God listens to us; but whoever is not from God does not listen to us. This is how we recognize the Spirit of truth and the spirit of falsehood. Dear friends, let us love one another, for love comes from God. Everyone who loves has been born of God and knows God" (1 John 4:4-7).

*I am indebted to Dr. Jan Paulsen for the information about Jante-law. He referred to it in an unpublished paper on leadership presented at Cohutta Springs Adventist Center, Crandall, Georgia, March 14-16, 1994.

CHAPTER
Three

We Need Revival

L et's face it—we are Laodicea. We think we have it made; we don't realize that we fall far short of God's plan for us.

But God, who doesn't see as we see, who looks on the heart, not on outward appearances, knows our true condition. He, the faithful and true Witness, the Great Physician, diagnoses our case. "I know your deeds," He says, "that you are neither cold nor hot. I wish you were either one or the other! So, because you are lukewarm—neither hot nor cold—I am about to spit you out of my mouth. You say, 'I am rich; I have acquired wealth and do not need a thing.' But you do not realize that you are wretched, pitiful, poor, blind, and naked" (Revelation 3:14-17).

Ellen White had it right: "A revival of true godliness among us is the greatest and most urgent of all our needs. To seek this should be our first work" (*Selected Messages*, 1:121).

We make high profession—we claim to be Adventists, people who expect and long for Jesus to return. But so often how we live denies what we say.

The Seventh-day Adventist Church needs reformation, and because it does, "reform" groups among us—as they like to call themselves—find a hearing. Many of our people are troubled by what they perceive to be the low spiritual state of the church, and the call for the church to come up higher strikes a responsive chord. But the message of revival goes beyond exhortation within the structure—the would-be reformers organize separate camp meetings and print their own papers. They have gone a long way down the road that leads to fragmentation.

Now, the mere fact that someone claims to be raised up by the Lord to give the "straight testimony" by no means ensures that he or she is of the Lord. It's always easier to condemn others, to point out the flaws of the church, than to give a positive message. A person or group may claim the divine unction, but the fruits of their ministry will provide the crucial evidence of God's presence in their work.

Simply claiming that one has the word of the Lord for this time is not sufficient. Scripture alone must be the test. Just as in Paul's day some who professed to bring the gospel preached not the gospel but a false gospel (see Galatians 1:6-9), so today, the call for reform may be bathed in a mixture of truth and error.

Likewise with Ellen White's writings. Copious quotations from her works may lead readers and hearers to believe that here, surely, are the true messengers for this time. Watch out! The devil quotes Scripture at will, for his purposes. The question isn't whether a person quotes the Bible or not, but whether he or she is truly *biblical*—that is, in harmony with the spirit and attitudes of Scripture. And with Ellen White's writings, the issue isn't whether someone quotes them little or much, but whether the message and ministry run in concert with the total counsel of her work.

We will take a hard look at the reformation of the church—what needs to change and how that can happen—in this chapter. But the point I am making is that the would-be "reformers" among us wouldn't get a hearing if the church were all that it ought to be. Part of what they are saying—their stern rebukes—strikes home among earnest souls who "sigh and cry" for the low spiritual state of God's people.

It's true—some amazing and shocking things are happening among Seventh-day Adventists. An elder sent to jail for committing incest with his daughter. A pastor who burns down his own (yes, Seventh-day Adventist!) church. Another pastor who gets involved in armed robbery. I never saw the likes of such things—in the world, yes, but not in my church!

Clifford Goldstein has listed more of these "horror stories" and wrestled with the question of how we can claim to be the remnant in light of them. His book *The Remnant* deserves careful consideration (Pacific Press Publishing Association, 1994).

At the *Adventist Review,* we choose not to print these "horror stories." Why? Not because we try to withhold information from the people but because they do not represent a true picture of the Seventh-day Adventist Church. The minister who goes crazy and burns down his church—that is an individual, not the Adventist ministry. And the elder in jail—he is an oddity, an aberration from the thousands of solid, sturdy, loyal men and women who provide leadership at the local church level. When a problem has national and international ramifications, like the Harris Pine bankruptcy or the Davenport losses, we will take it up in the *Review.* But we have too much good news to share to give our space over to the failures of scattered individuals.

The "reform" groups play up these problems, however. That is something you can put your money on with all of them—they specialize in pointing the finger. Somehow they have forgotten Paul's counsel that "love does not keep account of evil" (1 Corinthians 13:6, Phillips), because that is what they do. If the church tries to face up to the problem of our young people drinking in college, for instance, the "reformers" seize on the numbers and parade them as evidence of the church's terrible decline rather than working with leaders to help our youth put alcohol aside.

Recently, an elder in Australia sent me a bundle of papers from "reformers" in that country. I hadn't even heard of most of the individuals or groups, but they all had the same negative spirit. All set themselves up, subtly or overtly (one group called its meetings the Loud Cry—not so subtle!), as the genuine over against the apostate, mainline Seventh-day Adventist Church.

One of these photocopied publications opened—in the same manner in each of the issues my brother sent me— with two pages of faultfinding. Item by item, paragraph after weary paragraph, the paper scanned church bulletins, reports of youth camps, etc. Any mention of the church holding a social event or of young people getting together to play a ballgame or, in fact, anything that suggested Adventists might have fun or a good time— might actually smile and laugh—was singled out as evidence of apostasy.

Spare me from any endeavor like that! That's not a work the Lord has laid on me! And I doubt very much whether He has laid it on any other!

And spare me from the attitude behind such a work. Is this what reformation is about? Not according to my Bible.

The Bible has a great deal to say about reformation, in both Old and New Testaments. Seems as though God's people all along have fallen short of the divine will for them. I recommend that each reader study through the biblical material on reformation—study the reforms of Josiah and Hezekiah, the calls to reform by prophets like Isaiah, Jeremiah, and Joel, and also the messages of John the Baptist and Jesus, both of whom were reformers. You will find the information enlightening!

34

We can't pursue that study here—it's not the theme of this book—but I want you to notice one aspect associated with the biblical call for reformation. Over and over, in both the Old and New Testament, I find that genuine reformation means a change in the way in which we relate to other people. It means a call to fairness, justice, and mercy in all our dealings, a cleaning up of our lives so that we treat every other person as a son or daughter of the living God.

One of the most striking passages sounding this theme is Isaiah 58, that marvelous chapter we Adventists like to quote because it talks about the restoration of the Sabbath. But the whole passage is really about reform—false and genuine.

Verses 2 to 6 describe proposed reform. The people seek out God as though eager to know His ways; they appear to be commandment keepers; they fast and pray, lying in sackcloth and ashes. But God takes no account of their religious activity, because He sees it as a game. "On the day of your fasting, you do as you please and exploit all your workers," He says. "Your fasting ends in quarreling and strife, and in striking each other with wicked fists" (verses 3, 4).

The Lord then goes on to describe how genuine reformation reveals itself. "Is not this the fast that I choose: to loose the chains of injustice and untie the cords of the yoke, to set the oppressed free, and break every yoke? Is it not to share your food with the hungry, and to provide the poor wanderer with shelter—when you see the naked, to clothe him, and not to turn away from your own flesh and blood? . . . Then you will call, and the Lord will answer; you will cry for help, and he will say: Here am I. If you do away with the yoke of oppression, with the pointing finger and malicious talk, and if you spend yourselves in behalf of the hungry and satisfy the needs of the oppressed, then your light will rise in the darkness and your night will become like the noonday" (Isaiah 58:6-10).

Constantly the Hebrew prophets returned to the same themes. They challenged God's people to rend their hearts, not their garments (see Joel 2:13), to change the way they lived, not just their words. The little book of Micah captures biblical reformation in a verse that is the high-water mark of the Old Testament: "He has showed you, O man, what is good. And what does the Lord require of you? To act justly and to love mercy, and to walk humbly with your God" (Micah 6:8).

In the New Testament, we immediately meet a rugged reformer, the man from the desert: "Repent, for the kingdom of heaven is near," cries John the Baptist to the crowds who come out to hear him (Matthew 3:2). But for the so-called religious people, the Pharisees and Sadducees, he has a stern rebuke: "You brood of vipers! Who warned you to flee from the coming wrath? Produce fruit in keeping with repentance" (verses 7, 8).

And, like Isaiah and the other prophets before him, he called for a life of fairness, honesty, and justice. "The man with two tunics should share with him who has none, and the one who has food should do the same," he said. "Don't collect more than you are required to," he counseled the tax collectors, who were notorious for robbing the people. And to the soldiers: "Don't extort money and don't accuse people falsely—be content with your pay" (Luke 3:11-14).

This is biblical reformation. It cleans up our relationships with others, transforms all our dealings with other people.

And that was Jesus' call also. He began His ministry with the same words of reform John had used: "Repent, for the kingdom of heaven is near" (Matthew 4:17). But He soon elaborated what that kingdom is like: His Sermon on the Mount (Matthew 5–7) is the magna carta of the kingdom of heaven.

You can rightly translate "kingdom," the Greek *basilea*, by "rule" or "reign." Jesus described what happens when God's rule breaks through on earth, when men and women let Him be Lord of their lives—yes, even now, before the kingdom comes in glory. The children of the kingdom, He said, put God first, but they don't neglect the world of human relationships. Rather, they transform this world: they are merciful and peacemakers, changing society like salt and light. Their righteousness isn't seen in religious scrupulosity like that of the scribes and Pharisees. It far exceeds theirs, stretching to the thoughts and intents of the heart in all their dealings with other people.

The children of the kingdom, those in whose lives Jesus now reigns as king—they are a different breed. Not by blood, but by His indwelling presence. They belong to Him, and their lives reflect His life of gentle and loving deeds, His passion for purity, honesty, and justice.

This is what true reformation means, reformation that the Bible describes.

Strange, as I read the papers of the "reformers" among us, I don't find these themes. They seem to have a list of do's and don'ts they have put together from somewhere but are strangely silent on the great reform emphasis that runs throughout Scripture.

Certainly the church needs a reformation. But it needs to be a biblical reformation, not just a return to someone's recollection of what the church used to be like.

We have fallen far from the "good old days," right? The church of forty years ago—it was way more spiritual, right?

Not so fast! The Lord alone can make that call. I know enough, however, to tell you that the church of forty years ago was both better and worse than today's church.

It was better in that more Adventists probably studied

their Bibles faithfully, attended church regularly, and took their religion seriously. Fewer Adventist marriages ended in divorce, and more Adventist parents probably supported Christian education.

But listen, it was worse in other respects. If you were a black Adventist, you couldn't worship with many white congregations. You couldn't get treated at some white Adventist hospitals, nor could you attend many white colleges. And even though you worked in the General Conference, you had to eat by yourself, separate from the white brethren.

Unbelievable, but true! I weep for the cruelty, the injustice of my church of only forty years ago. If anyone tells you the church was better back then, tell them to open their eyes! I don't want to go back to the Adventist Church of forty years ago! That church needed reforming in the most desperate way.

All right, let's go back a century, to the 1890s. Surely the Adventist Church then was way ahead of the church today.

Maybe, maybe not. Ellen White had plenty to say about the corruption at church headquarters in Battle Creek. The power game played by a small group of men who controlled the whole church. The injustices done to workers and writers by the Review and Herald Publishing Association.

And those brothers and sisters had problems with sins of the flesh also. Adultery. Incest. Sexual abuse. Ellen White laid God's standard of reform right on the line.

So only the Lord knows how we compare with the old days. Don't call them "the good old days" unless you also call them "the bad old days"—because that's what they were.

The point is, God's people have *always* needed reformation. In Old Testament times. In New Testament times. A century ago. Forty years ago.

And today.

Repentance isn't a once-for-all act. It's a continual turning back to God, a leaving the world and its ways and a returning to the One who loves us so much.

Yes, a revival of true godliness among us is the greatest and most urgent of all our needs. We need Christ as the center of our lives and of the church. We need to turn away from material things and secular ways of thinking and return to Him. "The world is too much with us," wrote the poet Wordsworth. How true!

We need to return to the Bible, to be men and women of the Book once again. We need to feed on the Book, preach from the Book, and live by the Book.

And we need those divine remedies for our Laodicean lukewarmness—gold refined in the fire, white clothes, and eye salve (see Revelation 3:18). Faith that works by love—a life of loving service, like Jesus! The robe of His righteousness, in which there isn't one thread of human devising. The oil of the Holy Spirit to open our eyes so that we can see the beauty of the Lord, our own desperate need of Him, and the needs of a dying world.

Integrity, honesty, justice, mercy—these characteristics mark genuine reformation. Do we need them today? Absolutely. We need a revival that will bring our lives into concert with the divine pattern.

I get a lot of mail and over the years have seen such a variety that I didn't think I would be surprised by anything new. But recently I received a shocker.

The writer was responding to an article on changing patterns of church finances. He or she put the blame squarely on the blacks! "White's [sic] see their way of life under attack as never before and they see a church and government partially to blame for the problem. You see, Anglo-Saxons may not be the most vocal group but they send a message via their pocket-book. . . . Whites are pulling their wagons into a circle because of the attacks against our culture. We are not going to support a wild, charismatic, Africanized Church. . . . We no longer have a vision of bringing civilization or Christianity to the darker races because in the eyes of Whites they don't want it. We will do well to save it for our own children."

Whew! I have never read more racist writing anywhere. Not surprisingly, the writer didn't give a name.

Do we need biblical reformation? With attitudes like this around, we have a long way to go still.

We began this chapter by noting that "reformers" among us find support among some earnest Adventists. Will these "reformers" split the church? In a chapter 6 we will come back to these groups and attempt an answer.

Four

Generational Differences

There's nothing new about the generation gap—it's as old as the Bible.

We read there about a brash young man who was about to ascend the throne. Solomon, wealthiest and wisest of Israel's kings, had died, and now the nation gathered for the coronation of his son Rehoboam. But the people came with grievances. Solomon's massive building projects had come at a price, and they wanted relief from the heavy taxes. (Does that sound familiar?) "Your father put a heavy yoke on us, but now lighten the harsh labor and the heavy yoke he put on us, and we will serve you," they told Rehoboam (1 Kings 12:4).

So Rehoboam went to the elders from his father's era. "Give them what they want," they advised. "Tell them what they want to hear."

But Rehoboam wasn't impressed by these old geezers. He turned for counsel to the young men of his own generation—and they had something different to suggest. "Let the people know who's boss," they counseled. "Take charge. Crack the whip. You are king now, so let them have it."

When the people assembled three days later, the king spoke to them harshly. "My father made your yoke heavy," he thundered. "I will make it even heavier. My father scourged you with whips, I will scourge you with scorpions" (verse 14).

It was a classic example of bad communication. Ten tribes revolted and split off to form their own nation. They stoned the emissary Rehoboam sent to deal with them, and the king himself had to flee for his life.

Just like today: the younger generation wants to do it one way, the older generation a different way.

Ever see Mother and Daughter shopping for clothes in the mall? No matter what Mother chooses, it will be disgusting, embarrassing, horrible, and wrong, wrong, wrong. The best chance Mother has of getting Daughter to grudgingly accept an item is for her to say how terrible, unattractive, etc., etc., it is!

Ever wonder why "liberal" parents' children shock them by growing up so "conservative," or why "conservative" parents' kids turn out to embarrass their parents because of their "liberal" views?

The generations! They have gone different ways for as long as recorded history.

Today, however, the gap has widened to a chasm. This is because the family structure that sustained society and mitigated generational differences has fallen apart.

For millennia children grew up in contact with at least three generations in the family. Often children, parents, and grandparents lived under the same roof; if not, it was only across the meadows and through the woods to Grandmother's house.

Today, in the United States, very few families have grandparents in the home. More than half of all mothers with infants work outside the home. With divorce widespread, parental patterns and relationships have become confused.

Without interaction between the generations, relationships have fractured. Each generation has its own lingo, heroes, music, values. More and more, each generation talks to those of its own and finds all others incomprehensible, not worth the effort of trying to communicate. Lack of communication breeds misunderstanding, and misunderstanding, contempt.

Modern marketing philosophy exacerbates the differences. Television moguls are more concerned about *who* watches a particular show than *how many*. Advertising keeps the media in business, and companies target their products to specific audiences.

Look at the proliferation of magazines on the newsstand. They have become more and more specific, appealing to the interests of a particular age group, whether it be seventeen-year-old girls, working mothers, young professionals, or retired people. General magazines are struggling to survive: in this age of fragmentation, who will buy them?

William Strauss and Neil Howe, in their important work *Generations* (William Morrow, 1991), analyze the eighteen generations from the founding of America. They give particular study to the generations that have shaped and are shaping the twentieth century:

The "GI generation," born 1901 to 1924
The "Silent generation," born 1925 to 1942
The "Baby Boom generation," born 1943 to 1964
The "Baby Busters," born 1965 to 1985.
The "13th-ers," born 1986-

In the United States, the GI generation—the "can do" people who fought and won wars and gave the nation an incredible seven presidents—is in the throes of handing over the reins of power. The transition is anything but smooth. The GI generation is used to being in charge, to having things done its way. And even in retirement, they

43

wield massive political influence. They are suspicious of the upstart who displaced one of their own from the White House.

With the election of Bill Clinton, American politics skipped a generation. No one from the "Silent" generation (born 1925 to 1942) has made it to the presidency; presumably, no one will. Clinton, like Vice-President Al Gore, comes from the Baby Boomers, that huge seventy-five-million bubble that moves through time like the bulge in a python that swallowed a turkey.

Consider the images of the current occupants of the White House. Clinton in jogging shorts. Clinton in dark glasses playing the saxophone. Hillary Rodham Clinton as the first First Lady to present herself publicly as the intellectual equal of her husband.

From day one, Bill Clinton has faced a barrage of criticism. Surrounded by a retinue of young faces, he and his administration were expected to fail and therefore must fail. But with all the indecision and bumbling, through all the smoke, Clinton was winning major battles in Congress and forcing the nation to face critical issues that the presidents of the GI generation had neither the will nor the courage to tackle.

Depending on one's viewpoint, the Clinton presidency has been either a disaster or a badly needed change. It will take many years for a fair evaluation. I suspect that much of the criticism that has plagued the president will eventually be seen to be generational in origin.

And what of the church, our church, in this era of pronounced generational differences? In North America, and probably throughout much of the world, we reflect the patterns described above. The GI generation built up and ran the church. They worked hard, gave faithfully, sent their kids to Adventist schools, and kept the church going. They served as elders, deacons, Sabbath School leaders, and served on conference and union conference commit-tees. Many of them still lead the church.

I applaud the GI generation for their large role in maintaining, nurturing, and expanding the Seventh-day Adventist Church in North America. Their contribution to our corporate life surpasses that of those who came after—the Silent generation, to which I belong.

But the Seventh-day Adventist Church has a big prob-lem, in my judgment. By and large, the church hasn't passed on the torch to the Baby Boomers.

General Conference President Robert S. Folkenberg provides a glaring exception. Although he was born just outside the limits of the Baby Boom generation (he was born in 1941), he shows quintessential Boomer character-istics. A top-rated airplane pilot (yes, he is qualified to take over the controls if the captain of your commercial flight drops dead!), a helicopter pilot, a scuba diver, a computer whiz, a motorbike lover, he fits the mold. And he has brought to the General Conference a rash of new ideas and new initiatives that cut through the bureaucracy.

But few of Folkenberg's colleagues in the General Con-ference are as young as he. Nor does North America show a different pattern: leaders from the Baby Boom genera-tion are just beginning to assume conference presidencies. Overall, the Seventh-day Adventist Church in North America lags far behind society in handing over the reins from the GI generation.

All denominations suffered heavy losses of members among the Baby Boomers. This generation turned its back on many of the values of their elders. They weren't pre-pared to accept something merely because of its long tradition; they questioned everything, experimented, kept some items, rejected others. Their inquiries reached to the very nature of religion—and Christianity—itself.

Many Baby Boomers put off marriage, then put off

having children. But when they begin to raise families, many come back to church. But not necessarily the church of their childhood—they shop around to find a fellowship that seems right for them and especially for their kids.

I don't know of any data that bears on the topic, but my perception is that Adventists haven't done very well in attracting and holding Baby Boomers. Although we have suffered horrendous losses from this generation, many congregations seem unwilling to admit the problem or to make the effort to welcome and accommodate the needs of this group.

Will the Adventist Baby Boomers come back to the fold? There isn't much time left; the Boomers are turning fifty. And what about those who come back, perhaps after many years away, only to leave because they find the same old rigidity and lovelessness?

Because I am by nature incurably optimistic, I detest the way "crisis" is overplayed. But the church in North America may face a crisis in the years immediately ahead if the Baby Boom generation doesn't get on board. The GI generation has retired, and the Silent generation is retiring; who will take up the leadership and financial slack? We could be in for BIG problems.

These remarks about Baby Boomers in North America need to be qualified in two respects. First, we should beware of writing off the Boomers. We haven't lost an entire generation, as some people are claiming; if we had, our schools would have had to close years ago. That Adventist schools have kept operating demonstrates that many Boomers have stayed with the church. Further, Boomers have taken the lead in establishing new and growing congregations in several places. Unfortunately, we need many more involved Boomers.

Second, the problem we have been describing is largely confined to the white Adventist community. Blacks and

Hispanics have experienced much greater success in attracting and holding Boomers.

Apart from the special situation of the Baby Boomers, the church today reflects the generational differences of North American society. More and more, the children have their own worship service, as do the youth and the young adults. Singles go off on retreats, as do women, men (sometimes), and various other groups in the church such as the divorced, the bereaved, or the sexually abused.

The church is for ministry, and particular groups have particular needs. I support the diversification of ministry that enables more people of all ages and experiences to find fellowship, nurture, and worship. But how do we counteract this necessary segmentation so that it does not become fragmentation? How and when do we join hearts and voices as *one* body, one people in the Lord?

A recognition of generational differences can do much to remove misunderstanding and resolve conflict. Many items that divide congregations aren't questions of principle at all, no matter how much the protagonists want to claim this. Many are simply questions of likes and dislikes related to the respective generations.

Music probably causes more arguments than any other issue. Because I don't like a particular type of music or musical instrument, it's easy to pull in a moral or theological argument to try to boost my position. I will find it difficult to accept that someone else can be uplifted by what I think is cheap.

Now, I am not suggesting that just any music is appropriate for a worship situation, only that this whole area is so subjective that we all would do well to hold our peace and think carefully before we begin to accuse and condemn others. The Lord has used, and uses, a variety of types of music and musical instruments to His glory—from the psaltery, lyre, ram's horn, sackbut, flute, trumpet, and choral works of the Old Testament (which would sound strange to us) to popular tunes, even tavern songs, plucked from the streets and put to the praise of the Lord by Martin Luther, Charles Wesley, and others.

Another area where we see the generations diverging sharply is finances. Boomers are more selective in their giving patterns, less committed to loyal support of the church's programs. And they seem to view the matter of compensation for service in a different light. For many years the church has reimbursed its employees on the basis of a compressed wage scale that aims to meet the worker's essential needs—he or she should be able to live frugally at about the lower middle income level. Under this scale, differences in responsibility are reflected by only small differences in salary—for example, the General Conference president receives only slightly more than any other ordained minister in the North American Division.

For many Boomers, such a scale smacks of a socialistic philosophy and encourages mediocrity. They link compensation to performance and would extend the scale both up and down (many Boomers are driven men and women with high personal standards of professionalism who work extraordinarily hard and long—for large compensation).

For whatever reasons—perhaps under the impact of the Boomers—the church wage scale is falling apart in North America. It's full of holes and massive exceptions—college and university teachers are off it, and Adventist health care long ago abandoned it in favor of market rates.

Inevitably, these changes are causing reverberations. No subject gets people's attention like salaries! The horses are out of the barn, and they cannot be corralled. This matter seems bound to give rise to increased tensions among the church's employees in the days just ahead.

And there's one more aspect of these generational differences that threatens to fragment the church. Some matters are more than simply a question of taste, and I would hope that the older generations will be able to pass these values on to the church of the future. Some areas involve values that are worth preserving because they have made, and still make, an individual, church, or nation nobler and greater.

Honesty and integrity. Hard, faithful work. Thrift. Compassion. Service. Justice. Courage. Surely those of us who are older have a duty to instill and impart these virtues that cut across the generations.

A recent poll shows that 76 percent of respondents think that the United States is in a moral and spiritual decline. Not surprisingly, Bill Bennett's *The Book of Virtues* has sold more than a million copies in hardcover. And politicians are scrambling to jump on the "virtue" bandwagon. Adventists, with our heritage of morality and probity, surely have something to contribute to this debate!

The fragmentation of American society, however, shows no signs of abating. What about us—must our church reflect these trends? How can we begin hearing one another? How can we prevent the yawning gaps already present from shattering our oneness in Jesus Christ?

Five

Education:
Masterpiece or Monster?

S eventh-day Adventists had hardly organized into a legal body before they got into education. In 1872, just nine years after the General Conference was formed, we started our first school. From that humble beginning, we have developed a huge international network of 4,763 elementary schools, 939 secondary schools, and 81 colleges and universities.

Did we create a masterpiece or a monster?

Before I elaborate some of the problems education has brought, I want to make it perfectly clear that I am a supporter of Adventist education. I gave twenty years of my life to it, teaching at secondary, college, and graduate levels. My wife and I put both our children through Adventist schools right up through their baccalaureate degrees—which must have cost us plenty all told, although we have never tried to figure how much. Nor do we regret one penny of the expense. We *believed* in Adventist education and still believe. We believe that, with all their faults, our schools are the best place to send our children, because there the Christian option is at least given a chance.

Some people are down on Adventist education. They want our schools to correct what is happening in Adventist homes and churches, and because they do not, because

51

they cannot, these people bad-mouth Adventist education.

Other Adventists are hurting because children and grandchildren no longer are active in church life. Around North America I have discovered an enormous reservoir of pain and guilt over this loss. Parents and grandparents search the past to find out what they did or did not do that caused their young people to leave the church. And not a few blame our schools. They recall how they sent sons and daughters and grandsons and granddaughters off to academy or college, often at severe financial burden to themselves, hoping that they might become workers for the church or at least find an Adventist mate and loyally support the church in the local congregation. But instead, their children drifted into worldliness, divorce, and rejection of parental values.

The Adventist Church in North America is suffering staggering losses among its young people. How large the numbers are, nobody seems to know, nor are most leaders eager to know because the statistics would be discouraging. For many of our youth, their graduation from academy or college marks their "graduation" from church life also— they effectively drop out. Others move on to graduate school in a secular environment, make an effort to hold on to the church, but gradually slide into a tenuous relationship with Adventism or none at all.

Only the Lord knows all the factors that combine to make up this picture. It would be wrong to put the blame squarely on our schools—because our teachers are not spiritual or because they do not uphold Adventist standards or because the curriculum is no different from other schools. Let us admit that our teachers and schools are not all they might be, but also realize that the problem cuts far deeper: *the very nature of education itself carries with it risks.*

Ellen White wrote a great deal about education. She called for a reform and set forth a distinct philosophy that embraced not only formal study but the entire span of life. The work of true education, she said, is to restore the divine image in humanity (*Education*, 15, 16). And instead of the patterns of rote memorization and repetition common to various approaches to learning, our schools should teach young people "to be thinkers, and not mere reflectors of other men's thought" (ibid., 17).

By and large, Adventist education has tried to follow this counsel. Especially in our colleges and universities we have exposed Adventist youth to the broad sphere of knowledge with its alternatives to the Adventist philosophy of life. While presenting the Christian option, we have encouraged the students to think for themselves, to defend their position, to choose and to stand on their own feet.

And we have become victims of our own success. On the one hand, we can rejoice at the superior quality of product from our schools. Our graduates are making their mark in all areas of life; they stand out; they are rising to the top of the heap. Although by worldly standards our colleges and universities are small, we can feel proud for what they are accomplishing.

But—and there is the other hand. Our young people have studied and thought for themselves, and many have come up with different answers.

Not in theology—very few youth and young adults challenge the church on doctrine. They may question the relevance of some of our beliefs as they have been presented to them, but not the beliefs themselves.

Not in theology, but in some aspects of lifestyle. Young people have weighed our arguments and use of Scripture and come up with different conclusions.

In particular, they fault the Adventist dress code. Their difficulties with it begin in boarding academy and college, where, unfortunately, deans and teachers often fail to draw a sharp enough line between school rules and God's rules. (I know!—I began work for the church as an acad-

53

emy dean of boys.) They make young people feel that breaking the school rules is like committing sin, and they treat it the same. They fail to make clear that, while an institution has every right to formulate its own rules and dress code, the rules and the code in some respects are wholly arbitrary, without specific biblical basis.

In school and out of school, Adventist young adults have tested the dress code by Scripture, and some have found that it came up wanting. Their elders pointed to texts that forbade jewelry, for instance; they could find other passages that seemed to run in the opposite direction. And beyond that, they found inconsistency: adults could make a big issue out of the wedding band or a bracelet but wear gold tie clasps and watches and drive home from church in their Mercedes-Benz or Cadillac automobiles.

In today's church in North America, you can find wide differences in how Adventists dress and adorn themselves. Many saints are shocked by what they see, but many saints are not.

Worldwide, you will meet even greater differences in lifestyle among Adventists. Sabbath observance between Europe and North America, as well as within North America, varies greatly. Some Adventists visiting Europe from the States are shocked by what seems to them lax Sabbath behavior, but the Europeans come to America and are equally shocked by the materialism and adornment of Adventists here!

Some Adventists think fellow believers should look and live and worship the same everywhere in the world. What that comes down to is that they should look and live like American Seventh-day Adventists! In fact, the dress, food, music, and culture among the more than two hundred nations from which Adventists now come make mockery of any such misguided attempts at uniformity. Vegetarian diet is the ideal, but the church does not try to impose that on South Sea islanders, who exist on coconuts and fish, with Linkettes and Vegeburgers neither accessible nor affordable. In North India, modest dress for a woman dictates that she wear, not a dress, but an outfit with pants. And around the Pacific Rim, across Southern Asia and throughout Africa, the sounds of worship come, not only in languages other than English, but in different melodies, different form, and accompanied by different instruments.

From a human perspective, the effort to preserve Adventists as a worldwide people with a distinctive lifestyle is an impossible dream. But God loves that word *impossible*, because all things are possible with Him. And, despite the differences we have just mentioned, which are real and which we should not try to eliminate but rather cultivate as Adventism takes root in native soil, there *is* a oneness of Adventist lifestyle around the globe.

The Sabbath—the most distinctive lifestyle feature— unites us in practice. And Adventists care about healthful living: we avoid tobacco, alcohol, and drugs as we seek to honor God in all our living. It's a fact: Adventists simply look better than other people, look fitter, cleaner, happier. I have seen them in Papua New Guinea, have traveled by jeep from village to village along rutted tracks, and before long have been able to identify the Adventist villages without being told. No pigs. Happy, shining faces. Clean.

That is why I do not like the breaking down of the Adventist dress code in North America, Europe, and the South Pacific. Not because it is based on a couple of texts but because simplicity of life is a big virtue in my book. A people who live simply in all respects, not just in the way they dress and adorn themselves—I think that is a big plus, not only from a scriptural standpoint but also from the standpoint of environmental concern.

Another lifestyle area in which the church is fragmenting is that of entertainment, and in particular, the movies. The need to clean up our act is desperate. Despite our claim of high standards, we are in far worse shape than many evangelical Christians—their habits of movie and TV watching are far purer than ours.

The worst part of our situation is the paralysis of silence on the topic. For years we told our people: "Adventists don't go to movies," and we gave our reasons and tried to find texts to back them up. That is still our standard, but it has been massively rejected. Our old reasons no longer hold up: you don't have to go to movies, because the movies come into your home via TV or a rented video. And furthermore, our schools and churches screen movies to Adventist audiences. Conclusion: movies can't be bad *per se*, so the old approach of total avoidance doesn't wash.

The result is that many Adventists watch trash. They let the TV run on and entice them into sub-Christian and anti-Christian shows. They go to the movies to pass the time or rent a video with little thought as to its values. We need to learn how to select movies and programs that are appropriate for Christians. Our members could benefit from a critique of current movies and programs in terms of their values.

The evangelicals provide such education and critiques. We don't; we are caught in a paralysis of silence. The "standard" is out there still, and any movement along the lines that we so much need brings down the wrath of some of the saints because they think we have departed from the standard or are encouraging others to jettison it.

My conversations with Adventist young adults leads me to conclude that the church's double standard with regard to movies and TV is costing the church enormously in loss of credibility. To the younger generation, this is further evidence that the church isn't real, that it tries to live in some imaginary world from the past. Thus, this factor contributes to loss of interest in the church and what it stands for.

The focal point of this chapter isn't the movies or even lifestyle, however, but education. Is Adventist education to blame for the fragmentation we have been describing?

Only to the extent that our schools have encouraged our young people to test ideas and form their own conclusions. That is, to be thinkers, not mere reflectors of the thoughts of others.

We should mention a further point with regard to education, one that the church faced early in the twentieth century. Following instruction from Ellen White that Adventists should establish a medical institution in southern California and that it should prepare our youth to be physicians and nurses, the church founded the school known today as Loma Linda University. The turning point came early, when leaders asked Ellen White concerning the level of teaching for the new center. She replied that the instruction should be adequate to enable graduates to practice medicine.

Thereby, Adventists crossed the Rubicon. The preparation of fully qualified doctors demanded that the new school be accredited—with consequent implications for curriculum, faculty, and library.

Conceivably, Adventist education could have confined itself to a narrow circle. Our schools could have become Bible colleges, concentrating on a specialized, unique curriculum. But the Loma Linda development settled forever that question. One by one, all our colleges opted for accreditation, although the process was slow and resented by many, both on the campuses and at the General Conference.

Adventists took another big step when we decided to establish universities. The chain of events initiated by seeking accreditation now was repeated and intensified; the very concept of a university demands an openness to ideas, research, and a searching for truth. A church that owns and operates accredited colleges will be different from one that has only Bible colleges; a church that sets up

57

universities will be even more different.

I sometimes wonder: Did we realize what we were getting into when we decided to establish universities? Did our leaders foresee the opening to knowledge and questioning, with the possibilities of fragmentation, that would inevitably follow?

Some have questioned whether the very idea of an Adventist, or any Christian, university is viable, whether it is an oxymoron. I do not share this perspective. Every university operates with certain givens, within a particular environment. An Adventist university means that the quest for knowledge—which is the *sine qua non* of a university—proceeds from an Adventist philosophy of life and the universe.

Nor, on balance, do I regret the church's decision to establish universities. As a graduate of and former teacher at one of them, I have a healthy pride in the institutions and praise the Lord for what He has accomplished.

But the gains have come at a price. The Adventist experiment in education has resulted in a membership that is far better educated than the population around them, but it has also widened the gap between educated and less-educated Adventists in North America and between Adventists in the West and Adventists in developing countries. And in North America, where education as a system has developed the farthest, we face a sad pattern: people join the church, their children rise in society because of Adventist education, but in the next generation or so, the children, even better educated, cycle out of the church in large numbers.

Adventist education has enriched, and enriches, this movement to a remarkable degree. But it also has brought much greater variety among us, and as the quest for knowledge is pursued ever more rigorously, increasing fragmentation.

CHAPTER
Six

Modern Technology

Recently I was looking through bound copies of the *Review* from forty years ago and came across a long series by then-editor Francis D. Nichol. In these articles he lambasted various independent groups that were working among Adventists, seeking by one means or another to gain a following. Nichol didn't name anyone, but he listed the specific moral lapses and other failings of the leaders of these groups. His words were so pointed that readers in his day could hardly have failed to identify those whom he was exposing.

I had a strange sense of *de´jà vu* in reading these editorials. The charges these dissident elements leveled against the church and its leaders, and their method of approach, could be lifted right out of the pages of various privately published papers today. The names have changed, but little else.

What has changed is the technology available to the dissidents. The development of desktop publishing has given a new definition to the word *crank*. Through it, and through another invention—videotape and the VCR—the dissidents among us multiply their influence. Modern technology makes possible widespread dissemination of their ideas in attractive print or video packaging.

Now, I wholeheartedly support individualism and individual initiative. This is the spirit that founded our movement and has made it what it is. A century ago, and still today, anyone who is a strong Seventh-day Adventist will be a strong individual, a person prepared to swim against the popular tide. Even with the widespread five-day workweek and few hardships for Sabbath keepers, the fourth commandment still cuts across the grain of the world in shopping, sports, pleasures, and societal events.

Further, individual ministries accomplish great good. They spread the good news and build up the church in countless ways that the church, through its employees, could not. On the basis of the New Testament, I hold that every believer is a minister, that every member has a ministry that the Lord wants him or her to carry out. The church is for ministry—by *all* of us. Some of us are paid, and some of us are not, but we are all in this great task together.

I rejoice to see men and women dreaming dreams and putting their faith to work. I delight to see Adventist Frontier Missions, a lay organization, recruiting young people to go out into unentered areas. I applaud Maranatha Volunteers International and other such organizations that tap volunteers who give time, energy, and resources to construct churches and schools in various countries. I thrill at the energy and initiative displayed by members of Adventist Laymen's Services & Industries (ASI)—laypeople banded together to use their know-how to forward Jesus' great commission.

So, when I zero in on independent ministries in this chapter and elsewhere in this book, I want readers to understand that I am not criticizing those that work in a supporting way. The numbers of the latter are large; they build up the church and keep the wheels turning around the world. By contrast, a much smaller group of private ministries have turned inward—instead of helping a lost world that needs the everlasting gospel, they focus on the church and its failings. They have become supercritical and judgmental; they feel their mission is to rebuke the faults (as they perceive them) of Adventist leaders, ministers, colleges, hospitals, young people, etc., etc., etc.

If there were no Seventh-day Adventist Church in place, these people could not exist. They seek and use mailing lists of members; they prey upon the work built up by so many years of toil and tears. The word is a harsh one but accurate, so let us say it in love: They are parasites on the church, gaining their living from contributions from members who, for one reason or another, become persuaded by the publications or videos the independents send them.

Most of these dissident groups are very small, but you wouldn't know it by what they send you in the mail. Nor do they let you know from the outset their relation to the church. They *always* present themselves in the most favorable light, as loyal, fundamental, historic Seventh-day Adventists. Some will use the title "elder" or "pastor," though they have no credentials recognized by the church. Some fail to tell you that they *aren't even members of the Seventh-day Adventist Church!* They invite you to support them financially, but I have never seen an audit of their ministry or a public accounting of the use of the tithes and offerings that are sent them.

Frankly, I am amazed at the gullibility of some of my brothers and sisters in the faith. Incensed at supposed misuse of funds by church officials, they will send money to an independent group that has neither audit nor disclosure! Even if we grant that occasionally financial mistakes are made by the mainline church, at least the books are audited and leaders can be called to account!

And there's something else that amazes me, something that enables the dissidents to get a hearing for their literature. Too many Adventists seem to think that anything that appears in print comes with a measure of credibility. No matter that the material is a twisting of the truth or outright lies; if it's in print, you have to take it seriously!

That's absurd, of course. All you need to do to get something in print is to give it to a printer and pay his fee. Or, if you have your own computer, you can publish it yourself. No one is out there to check if your facts are straight. No one will alert the reader to "the rest of the story"—what you conveniently left out because it would change the picture completely. No one will stick on a warning label: "Readers, read with care. Don't believe it just because it comes in printed form."

Look at the garbage on the newsstand, in any bookstore. Here are hundreds of works in print—fiction, crazy stuff, evil stuff, imaginary stuff, as well as some worthwhile stuff. All in print, but most of it worthless and less than worthless (because it corrupts).

When, oh when, will our people learn to "test everything. Hold on to the good" (1 Thessalonians 5:21)? When will we learn to beware of literature that insinuates itself as genuinely Adventist when it isn't, that mixes the Spirit of Prophecy with the spirit of faultfinding, that erodes trust in leadership and the onward progress of the movement?

Here are two instances that illustrate the problem.

A leader in a certain conference came under attack by certain elements. He faced vilification in print and met with members from place to place in an effort to give them the facts. In one location, after he had exposed the published charges as utter fabrication—he was accused of activities when he wasn't even present—a sister replied, referring to the printed attacks: "But they couldn't have printed it if it wasn't true"!

Second example, which I saw for myself. Recently the president and entire religion faculty of Southern College were lambasted in a publication given out to constituents of the college. Anyone who knew the people under attack could hardly refrain from laughing out loud, so ridiculous were the charges. If these leaders and teachers were so "liberal" that they should resign (which is what the paper called for), so should just about every other leader in North America!

The college administration's response surprised me. I thought the paper didn't deserve any official notice, but the college prepared a counterpublication answering its charges and affirming support for the leaders and teachers. My immediate reaction was that the college overreacted, but before long, others on the scene set me straight. They told me that some good Adventists, reading the scurrilous paper, would conclude that maybe there was something to the accusations if they were not officially denied.

I am sorry that the college had to take this course of action. They probably did what was best under the circumstances, but I am sorry that Adventists could be so gullible.

In cases like these, we often hear the old "Where there's smoke there's fire" line. Maybe the picture isn't quite as bad as painted, but there's something there. Something not right. Something fishy.

Bad reasoning, that is. It's a variation of the "They wouldn't print it if it weren't true" argument. Where there's smoke, there may be fire. Or just smoke—nothing more, smoke that a critic is blowing in our faces.

Videos have amazing power to persuade, even beyond the printed page. Get a charismatic speaker, drop in quotations from Ellen White displayed in the screen, add the name of Jesus and even prayer, and the mix can be potent for either good or evil. In the hands of a skillful manipulator, it can deceive even the saints.

Some time ago an earnest member, who happened to be one of my students long ago, called me and urged me to view a set of videos. I have many other uses for the little free time I get and tried to put him off, but he kept on calling. It was obvious that he felt the material was vital for me and the Seventh-day Adventist Church.

At last I relented and sat down to watch the two videos; it was a Sabbath evening. Before long, my Sabbath peace and rest were shattered. The material, presented so smoothly and, on the surface, so sincerely, was a farrago of truth, half-truth, innuendo, and accusation. The total blend, incorporating Bible and Ellen White references, manipulated the viewer.

I was angry. Angry because I could see what was going on beneath the pious exterior. Angry because I could spot misquotations of sources, twisting of the Spirit of Prophecy, false conclusions. And angry because I knew that many well-meaning folks would see these videos and be seduced by them.

After completing the first video, which ran for more than one hour, I had had enough. I felt contaminated; I refused to view the second one. All that Friday night I tossed and turned on my bed, amazed at the power of deception, grieving for the impact on gullible brothers and sisters.

The next week I returned the videos to the man who had urged them upon me. In no uncertain terms, I warned him to be on his guard in viewing them and appealed to him to consider his course of action in sharing them with others.

I will not attempt to judge the motives of those who produce such videos and publications. The Lord knows; I do not need to know. But for whatever reasons, they have become engaged in a work whose fruit is criticism, fault-finding, judgmentalism, and negativism. Jesus said: "By their fruits ye shall know them" (Matthew 7:16, KJV), and the fruits make clear that the work is not from God.

The most difficult form of error we have to meet is the one that comes mixed with truth. If these independents broke away and started a new denomination, they'd pose very little problem. Our people would recognize them for what they are and have nothing to do with them. Or if they renounced the writings of Ellen White or rejected the foundational truths of our message, they would be exposed. But they don't: they come in the garb of teachers of truth, those who adhere to the old ways in the midst of the church's apostasy.

In fact, these people are directly out of line with one of the fundamental beliefs of the Seventh-day Adventist Church. Among our twenty-seven cardinal teachings, you find not only Jesus, Creation, the second coming, the Sabbath, the sanctuary, and so on, but also number 13—"Unity in the Body of Christ." By attacking the church, its ministry, leadership, and conduct, the dissidents deny this fundamental belief. By appropriating tithes and offerings for themselves, by holding their own worship services and camp meetings, by (in some cases) ordaining their own clergy without authorization, they weaken the Body just as surely as if they denied the Sabbath or the second coming.

Over the years, I have seen the dissidents at work. A classmate in the ministerial course at Avondale College was one Robert Brinsmead. Even then, he had his own ideas; even then, he worked to build a following. Alarmed at what they were observing, the faculty of the college refused to register him for his senior year unless he would give signed assurances. But Bob would not, so he never graduated with me. He went off on a tangent with his Sanctuary Awakening Fellowship (of course, it had a paper!), only to switch gears suddenly a decade later and eventually to part completely with the Seventh-day Adventist Church.

Before I sorted out Brinsmead's theology—his ideas about perfection, the papacy making inroads into the church, and the flesh of Christ—I had sorted out his spirit. I knew in myself that the attitudes that were driving him were not for me, no matter how attractive his ideas might sound and how much he might quote from Ellen White.

That was nearly forty years ago. Brinsmead is a name remembered only by those who have been around awhile. The saddest part is that good people—especially earnest, new converts, and some pastors—got caught up with him. He went his way; they lost their way.

The mix of truth and error still attracts people today. Sometimes it takes years for them to realize where the ideas are headed. Some people perhaps never really see the big picture; but praise God, some do and make a U-turn.

Here's what the mail brought us one day:

"About 1985, when I was 30 years old, the Holy Spirit began to draw me into a closer personal relationship with Jesus. I had grown up in our church, and am SDA educated, but never really had a relationship with Jesus. Well I began to listen and hear for the first time in my heart. I subscribed to the *Review* and began to read it cover to cover. I soon found that I was in love with my God, my church, and even the *Review!* I was a sponge and soaked it all in.

"In time my family and I moved to another state for my husband to take further training for his work. While we were there I found, to my dismay, that I wasn't getting the same kind of spiritual nourishment at church that I had before. I felt so empty after the Sabbath worship service. I prayed about it, but it didn't get any better. Later I came across the *Our Firm Foundation* magazine. I read it and it seemed to fill the void I was experiencing. In due time I subscribed.

"Over the next two years I experienced a growing uneasiness. I found myself to be suspicious of my church. I

66

listened to my pastor but was afraid of what his sermons were teaching. I was afraid of what my children were being taught in their SDA church school. I even thought the *Adventist Review* was lacking in content and not 'preaching the word'!

"We'd moved again, but I was miserable. I still loved God of course, and the church, but I was so afraid, suspicious, and critical! I prayed about it and felt it had something to do with the magazine I was reading. In talking to God about it, He reminded me that 'by their fruits you shall know them.' But I didn't know those editors, so how could I know their fruits? Then, by way of a cassette tape of a seminar series I was listening to, God revealed to me that *their* fruits will be manifested in my life when I partake of their message. So, I could see that my distrust and suspicions were the result—the fruit—of what I was reading.

"It was a struggle, but in a couple of months I was free of those thoughts, and no longer read that publication. I praise God for seeing me through that trial.

"And now? I'm still in love with my Saviour, my church, and the *Adventist Review* has regained its place in my esteem.

"Thank you for the courage to come to the front and print what may not always be popular. Keep it up!"

Chances are, we'll have the dissidents with us until the Lord comes. Their potential to fragment the church is greater than ever before because modern technology multiplies their influence.

How shall we deal with them?

With patience—which only the Lord can supply. The energies of pastors and administrators drain away in trying to put out fires kindled by the dissidents; the temptation is to get angry and call for a clean-out. That course of action is always dangerous, because we may uproot the wheat along with the tares.

With love—which only the Lord can supply. People *can* change and *do* change. Yes, even those who once seemed so steeped in the acid of faultfinding that no change was possible.

And with wisdom—which only the Lord can supply. There is a time to be silent and a time to speak out, to tell the people the facts, to name names and give reasons. There is a time to work quietly and a time to act decisively in order that the Body not be weakened further by attack upon it.

Only God can help us to know what is the right course of action for the time.

CHAPTER Seven

Frustration Over the "Delay"

Why are we still here? That's the question eating at the spiritual vitals of many Seventh-day Adventists.

We are still here. More than 150 years have passed since William Miller and the other Adventists expected Jesus to come on October 22, 1844. Our movement originated in that "great disappointment," in the small band of believers who didn't—like the great majority of the Millerites—abandon belief in the imminent return of Jesus. They continued to preach that Jesus was coming, and coming soon. He had entered the Most Holy Place of the heavenly sanctuary, and His work there—the investigative judgment—would soon be done, and He would come to earth in the second advent.

Those of us who grew up in the church have heard scores of sermons on the second advent. We have heard pastors and evangelists pointing out the "signs" that show that Jesus is "at the door, yes, even at the door." We have grown old in the expectation of the advent.

And we are still here. Many of us are disappointed. The way preachers presented the second coming, we were sure Jesus would have come long ago. But He didn't, and while we don't feel quite as bad as Hiram Edson, who, looking back on the great disappointment, wrote: "We wept and wept until the day dawn," we do feel let down. How much longer do we have to wait?

And some of us go farther. We are concerned to find out *why* Jesus hasn't come yet. We come up with various answers, and some of them involve what Adventists need to *do* in order for Jesus to return.

The various people who attempt to explain why Jesus hasn't come don't agree in their findings. But some of the "explanations" are deadly serious—after all, if *we* are responsible for Jesus' "delay," then we need to know. This should become the most important and urgent item on the church's agenda.

So, within the ranks of Seventh-day Adventists, you can find not only the fundamental belief that Jesus will come a second time, but teachings that go much beyond this pillar doctrine. These teachings all attempt to tell us *why* Jesus hasn't come yet.

What do the theologies of Herbert Douglass and Desmond Ford have in common? Not much on the surface, but, in fact, both attempt to deal with the same point—the "delay" in the second coming. Likewise those of Jack Sequeira and Ralph Larson: apparently so different, they take up the same question. I could add other names, but my purpose here isn't to dissect the teachings of any individual, merely to show how the question is a powerful one for leading Adventist thinkers.

Put yourself in the shoes of John and Mary Doe, who have recently joined the church. They attended meetings held by an Adventist minister who presented the "blessed hope" in a winsome, biblical fashion. John and Mary listened attentively, and the thought of Jesus' soon return captivated their hearts. As they studied the Scriptures to know more about the people of the advent—the Adventists—they decided to cast in their lot with them.

Soon they are in the local church, voted into fellowship

after their baptism—and what a change! In the evangelistic meetings, the teachings of the second advent shone bright and clear, simple and certain. Now they begin to encounter ideas they hadn't heard in their Bible studies before baptism. Some are in books published by the church presses; other come from private magazines.

And John and Mary begin to feel confused about the second coming. What started out as the "blessed hope" doesn't seem so blessed in some of the things they read—it puts a guilt trip on them. And rather than uniting Adventists in joyful expectation, it seems to have become a source of fragmentation.

Is the above scenario true or false? In many Seventh-day Adventist churches, unfortunately, it is true. The doctrine that is so basic that it's part of our name—we are Seventh-day *Adventists*—is being obscured by theological debate.

With Adventists writing complete books on the topic of the "delay," I cannot begin to deal with it adequately in one chapter. Nor is it my purpose in this book to try to solve all our problems—I am attempting to lay out the factors that divide or would divide us and point the way beyond them.

In the remainder of this chapter, therefore, I shall list the three main responses I have observed to the apparent delay in the second coming and give my view of each. Finally, I shall note several observations that I believe bear on the whole subject of the "delay." Although my remarks will have to be brief, I hope they will clearly indicate my view of the biblical position in this important area.

Response 1: Eschatological burnout. Some members are so frustrated over the delay in Jesus' return that they are Adventists in name only. The hope of the soon return of Jesus no longer impacts their lives in a significant way.

Our opponents, of course, encourage this response. "Why don't you admit you were wrong?" they throw at us. "Come

71

on—150 years since 1844, and Jesus hasn't come! Why don't you give up these ideas?"

That's the course taken by the mainline churches. Every Sunday they may still recite the Apostles' Creed with its line about Jesus' coming "to judge the quick and the dead," but long ago they quit thinking of the doctrine of the second coming as something meaningful to Christian experience.

But I'm not abandoning belief in the second coming! I'm not about to relegate it to the back shelf of my life! I believe the words of Jesus, and He promised: "I will come again"! (John 14:1-3, KJV). Every writer of the New Testament believed that promise, and it motivated the New Testament church. Anyone who takes the Bible seriously just has to be an Adventist—it sticks out a mile.

How tragic that the hope of the advent should burn low in the lives of some Seventh-day Adventists! How tragic that some Seventh-day Adventist preachers should feel so uncertain or embarrassed that they no longer preach about it!

But there's a second response—and just the opposite of the first one.

Response 2: Eschatological fever. If some Adventists feel burned out on the second coming, others are white hot in calculating *when* He'll return. They have their charts, their calendars, and their reasoning and, by specific dates or implied dates, they tell us that Jesus must come very soon.

At the *Review* office we get a lot of these materials. Not surprisingly: if someone has discovered that the final events of this world's history will all wrap up within, say, three years, that's a message that the church needs to share, and share urgently.

I remember well a telephone conversation of several years ago. This brother whom I did not know, a professional living on the West Coast of the United States, had

72

something he wanted to show me. He wouldn't disclose details, merely that he was ready to get on an airplane and fly to the General Conference to present it to me so that I could put it in the *Adventist Review*.

I counseled him to save the airfare. Besides, I had a conference to attend in his area after a short time; why not set up an appointment when we could get together?

So we did. One evening he arrived, briefcase in hand, at the motel where I was staying. He took out a series of papers and a large chart intersected by lines, dates, and events. For a couple of hours, he led me through his reasoning, which was convoluted. But the bottom line of it all—the key idea derived from the Hebrew and Egyptian calendars, jubilee cycles, prophecy, and parables—was that Jesus would return in May that year. And it was already late in January!

Now, I need to stress that this man was sincere and kind in his convictions. He presented his ideas with deep concern but in a spirit of sharing, of wanting input from others. He did not subsequently publish them abroad.

I told him that I saw no light in his calculations. I warned him about the error of attempting to set a date for the second coming. But I let him know that I appreciated the spirit he manifested. And as we parted, I said, "I hope you are right. Maybe we will meet again soon—in May!"

I wish that others who feel motivated to calculate the dates for last-day events would manifest the same spirit. Unfortunately, I encounter a rash of materials from all sides warning us, startling us, terrorizing us. Some of the publications come from Seventh-day Adventist writers and employ the jubilee cycle as a key element; some come from fundamentalist-evangelical groups who place great weight on 1948, the year of the founding of the modern state of Israel, and some even come from Roman Catholic sources with purported visions from the Virgin Mary about the end-time calamities that are about to transpire.

But Jesus said, referring to the second coming: "No one knows about that day or hour, not even the angels in heaven, nor the Son, but only the Father" (Matthew 24:36). After His resurrection, the disciples inquired: "Lord, are you at this time going to restore the kingdom to Israel?" His response: "It is not for you to know the times or dates the Father has set by his own authority" (Acts 1:6, 7).

Ellen White preached on this passage—Acts 1:6, 7—in a sermon at Lansing, Michigan, in 1891. As she had consistently counseled throughout her long ministry whenever Adventists began to get excited over dates for the second coming, she again warned against all such calculations. In effect, she said we have more important ways to spend our efforts—to live every day for the glory of the Master by building up His kingdom. And her words are still worth remembering in our days more than one hundred years later: "You will not be able to say that He will come in one, two, or five years, neither are you to put off His coming by stating that it may not be for ten or twenty years" (*Selected Messages*, 1:189).

Eschatological fever draws a crowd and sells books. But it is unbiblical and irresponsible, because ultimately it leads to eschatological burnout after the dates pass without Jesus' return.

Response 3: Eschatological theology. Eschatology, the doctrine of the last things, is a time-honored category of biblical theology. We Adventists have revived it after centuries of large-scale neglect, in particular, showing how the great time prophecies of Daniel and Revelation unfold the course of human history right down to the second coming and beyond. By "eschatological theology" here, I don't mean this general study of the end time but rather those theologies, not part of our twenty-seven

74

Fundamental Beliefs, that some Adventists have developed to explain why Jesus' coming is delayed.

I find two types of answers among these theologies of the "delay." Some focus on what we should do, others on what we should *preach.*

Those dealing with our actions zero in on either missionary work or character development. For the former, Matthew 24:14 is key: "And this gospel of the kingdom will be preached in the whole world as testimony to all nations, and then the end will come." Why hasn't Jesus come? Because the gospel hasn't gone to all humanity. So until it does—which means until we make greater efforts to spread it—His coming will be delayed.

For the latter (those focusing on the character of God's people), a passage like Revelation 14:1-5 is crucial. Here, John saw the 144,000 redeemed from the earth in the last days, and they are pure and blameless. Along with such scriptures, this statement of Ellen White plays a major role: "Christ is waiting with a longing desire for the manifestation of Himself in His church. When the character of Christ shall be perfectly reproduced in His people, then He will come to claim them as His own" (*Christ's Object Lessons*, 69).

This reasoning leads to what has become known as the "harvest principle": when, and only when the harvest is ready, will Jesus return. As interpreted by many who hold this point of view, it means that only when God's people (or a sufficient sample of those who profess Him) overcome sin and reflect the character of Jesus can Jesus come back for us.

These explanations for the delay run in different directions, but each ultimately puts the reason (blame?) for Jesus' "delay" squarely on us. Only when we clean up our act—whatever that means—can we expect to see Him coming in the clouds.

75

Other explanations, however, focus on our message for the world. The gospel of the kingdom is to go to all the world (that's Matthew 24:14), but what *is* the gospel? The first angel proclaims the everlasting gospel to every nation, kindred, tongue, and people, but just what does that everlasting gospel say?

So here the "answers" to the "delay" assert that we need to clean up our understanding of the gospel before Jesus can come. Only when we get the gospel straight and proclaim it can the world be enlightened with the glory of our Master and He will return.

Trouble is, the "answers" also part company over the meaning of the gospel. For some, it centers in justification; for others, in victory over sin in our personal lives. We will come back to this topic in more detail in chapter 10 of this book.

Back to our new members John and Mary Doe. What are they to make of all these ideas? Here is what I would point out:

1. From a biblical basis, those who talk about the "delay" in the second coming aren't the most desirable company for Adventists! We find this idea only a few times in the New Testament, and each time, it comes from those on the wrong side of the fence.

In one case Jesus told the story of the wicked servant, who, after his master has gone away, says to himself, "My lord delayeth his coming" and begins to beat up his fellow servants and hit the bottle (Matthew 24:48, 49, KJV).

In another case, both Peter and Jude warn us that in the last days, scoffers will cast scorn on the second coming. "They will say, 'Where is this "coming" he promised? Ever since our fathers died, everything goes on as it has since the beginning of creation' " (2 Peter 3:3, 4).

So it isn't true followers of Jesus, but the careless and defiant, who focus on the "delay" in the second coming!

Now, I don't suggest that those Adventists who write and speak extensively on this subject belong in that camp, but, merely suggest that the biblical evidence certainly doesn't encourage us in such efforts.

2. Nor does the Bible support the idea that humans can frustrate God's plan. To the contrary: the Scriptures portray God as Lord of time and space, working out His sovereign will unchecked. They tell us that Christ came the first time "when the time had fully come" (Galatians 4:4)—right on God's time. We may conclude that His second coming will also be according to the divine timetable.

Only one text in all of Scripture contains the thought that humans may affect the time for the second coming. This is 2 Peter 3:11, 12, which reads: "Since everything will be destroyed in this way, what kind of people ought you to be? You ought to live holy and godly lives as you look forward to the day of God and speed its coming. That day will bring about the destruction of the heavens by fire, and the elements will melt in the heat." However, the ancient manuscripts are divided in the reading of this passage, with many to be translated as "as you *wait eagerly* for the day of God to come" instead of "speed its coming." Even if "speed its coming" is correct, however, we should note that it does not speak of our *delaying* the second coming but rather hastening it. The Bible nowhere suggests that we can delay the advent.

3. In God's plan, humanity and divinity cooperate. God hasn't committed the work of the gospel to angels but to us; further, when Jesus comes, there *will* be a people ready to meet Him and to live with Him forever. We have a part to play, but ultimately, God is in charge. Because He is King of kings and Lord of lords, all things must come to pass according to His timetable.

Ellen White expresses the same thought: "Like the stars in the vast circuit of their appointed path, God's purposes know no haste and no delay" (*The Desire of Ages*, 32).

4. In doing theology, we must always be sure that we begin with the Center, Jesus. Jesus in His being as truly God and truly human, Jesus as Saviour and Lord—He alone must form the focus for all other thought. With Him at the center, we can move to other subjects, including eschatology.

But if we start with eschatology, we run the risk of aberrant theology—we are starting where we should be finishing. Unfortunately, some Adventists have fallen into that rut. Some begin with eschatology and move *back* to Christology—the doctrine of Jesus. No wonder their ideas cannot pass the biblical test.

The second coming, a fragmenting factor? Yes—impossible, but true. Not because of the doctrine itself but because of its misuse and misapplication.

Let's get back to the Bible. Let's make the Bible central and foundational. Then Jesus' return will shine forth again as the "blessed hope" that will unite us, not divide.

Eight

Amazing Growth

Here is another area where we have become a victim of our own success. The vision of Revelation 14:6,7 is being realized in our day, as the everlasting gospel goes forward with ever-increasing power to every nation under heaven.

But this growth creates tremendous tensions for a church that seeks to continue as one body, a united communion. I will focus on two areas of tension—money and race.

The more the church grows in underdeveloped areas, the greater the strain on the Adventist dollar. The traditional "home bases"—North America, Western Europe, Australia, and New Zealand—find themselves increasingly strapped for funds. And the situation becomes heightened with every passing day.

Just look at the numbers—they jump out at us:

•fifty years ago, our total membership was less than 600,000; today, it is more than eight million.

•fifty years ago, North America made up 37 percent of total membership; today, only 10.1 percent.

•fifty years ago, Europe counted for 22 percent of Adventists; today, only 3.8 percent.

On the other hand:

• fifty years ago, Latin America supplied only 16 percent of world membership; today, 34 percent.

• fifty years ago, Africa comprised 10 percent; but today, 32 percent.

So the balance has swung dramatically. Only fifty years ago, North America and Europe were in the majority, with 59 percent of the membership; today, they combine for only 14 percent. But Latin America and Africa together have moved from 26 percent to 66 percent.

And if you're surprised at these raw figures, fasten your seat belts. Let's look down the road a few years to A.D. 2000. Based on current trends, this is how our church will look:

• total membership, at least twelve million.

• members living in Africa, Latin America, and Asia, 86 percent.

• members living in North America and Europe, 10.5 percent.

Now you begin to understand why the job of treasurer, regardless of the level, has become more and more difficult. Because the church continues to grow much faster in the weaker financial areas than at "home," every year the budget gets harder and harder to balance.

A financial squeeze tests a person, a family, a nation, a church. When money runs short, it's easy to think and act selfishly, to begin blaming others, to resort to accusation and name-calling. Ugly tendencies—shameful prejudices that we thought were buried long ago—rise up from the grave.

Before we mention some of the negative consequences that confront us, let's be clear on two things:

First, the problems we are dealing with in this chapter

are the best sort to confront—they are problems of success. We should be glad for them and regard them not as problems but as challenges and opportunities. Think of all the prayers that ascended for more than a century that the Lord would "bless the mission fields." Well, He has answered those petitions in such an abundant fashion that we hardly know how to cope with the blessing. We should *rejoice* in the new situation, not look upon it in anxiety or frustration.

Second, the Lord continues to bless our church with multiplied financial resources. The squeeze we're experiencing and will continue to experience doesn't come from a drying up of the financial base. A few voices of gloom and doom among us want to suggest that the church is in decline, that the economic pressures we are learning to live with are due to falling confidence and falling support. No way! While it's true that giving patterns—tithe and offerings—have not kept pace with growth in the home bases, the overall financial picture remains bright. What we're talking about is giving that doesn't increase *fast enough* to cope with the tremendous growth of the church in less affluent parts of the world.

The annual budget of the General Conference—the monies it receives for disbursement among the eleven divisions of the world church and its own operations—is about $160 million. But that figure is only a small part of the total giving by Seventh-day Adventists. In North America, for example, annual tithe is more than $400 million plus other offerings. If we add up tithe and offerings for the worldwide church, the numbers every year exceed one billion dollars. And that doesn't include all the money that flows through our hospitals, clinics, universities, colleges, schools, publishing houses, literature-distribution systems, and health-food factories. Only the Lord knows what the total is, but it is very large.

81

When I think how we began, I am amazed and can only exclaim, "See what God has done!" (Numbers 23:23).

I think of Ellen White, only twenty years old (it was just a few days before her twenty-first birthday), receiving a vision in November 1848 that her husband James should start a little paper and that it would grow until the work would encompass the globe like streams of light. I think of the shock that instruction must have given James—he was homeless and penniless, a most unlikely candidate to start a worldwide endeavor. But he labored with his hands and gathered a few funds, and he wrote every word for the little paper, using a "library" that consisted of a Bible, a short version of *Cruden's Concordance*, and a dictionary with one cover off. By the summer of 1849, he was looking for a printer—a most unusual man, one who was prepared to wait for his payment until the paper went out and brought in contributions!

So, at last the paper was ready—one thousand copies of an eight-page tract, *The Present Truth*. The little band knelt around the copies, with supplication and tears, praying that the Lord would guide them into the hands of receptive readers. Then James put the papers in a carpet-bag and walked eight miles to the nearest post office.

The Seventh-day Adventist Church—not yet named as such (that would come eleven years later)—was on its way!

Let us never forget it: the work has always been short of funds. The movement has gone forward step by difficult step; the church has been built up brick by difficult brick. Toil, sweat, and tears have made it happen; and faith, earnest prayer, and vision. It's a story of multiplied miracles, some of which we know about but most recorded only by the angels in heaven.

In the Lord's providence and foreknowledge, He selected North America to be the womb of the movement. In this environment of freedom, abundant natural resources, and generosity, the church was cradled; here, it grew and prospered; and here to this day lies the financial base of a movement that has spread around the globe.

Only against this backdrop can we now take up the challenges of growth that we face today. To begin to paint the negative options without this larger picture from our past would make us the worst of ingrates.

But we do face negative options and will face them more and more as growth brings ever greater pressures. And each of these negatives, if they come about, will fragment the church.

The option of second-class citizenship. This would mean that we are content to live with wide disparities in opportunities for worship and personal growth. That Adventists in affluent societies retreat into a cocoon, turning a blind eye on the needs of their brothers and sisters in poorer lands.

Christianity isn't socialism—we shouldn't strive toward the impossible goal of bringing Adventists everywhere to the same economic level. Just as in any family some members will be more successful financially than others for a variety of reasons, so in the world Adventist family differences will remain among us until the Lord comes.

Granted this point, we must consider what is the acceptable limit of those differences. In certain respects it must simply be unacceptable to us all that some of us are deprived. The very fact that we are one people, one body, must motivate us all to efforts to make up for the lack of some. What are areas that should cause us to rally to help?

Obviously, conditions that threaten life itself. As I write, about one million Rwandians are refugees in Zaire. They have fled from the fighting and killing and are crowded into wretched, disease-ridden camps. Among them are more than one hundred thousand Adventists. The plight of all these refugees must stir us to help, and we must be especially concerned to aid our brothers and sisters in the faith.

Likewise, Adventists everywhere deserve at least minimal facilities for worship. They do not need a grand building and pipe organ, but they should have a roof over their heads. It should be unacceptable to the rest of us that congregations have to meet outside. But that is the case right now in Africa: more than two thousand congregations gather for worship in the open air because they don't have the $2,000 needed for galvanized roofing to complete their church buildings.

Third, every Adventist in the world should have access to basic information about the Christian life. Not a library of books, but elemental literature in the language of the people telling how to accept Christ, how to grow in Christ, and what Adventists believe.

Last, every Adventist child should have the opportunity for education. Education can help lift an individual and a community, but what a loss when no school is available! Who knows how much ability, how many gifts will never be developed for the betterment of society and the glory of the Lord?

Will we turn our backs on such basic needs? This is the negative option before us, and it will become ever more attractive as the numbers of Adventists continue to increase in the third world.

The option of the "haves" and the "have nots." As the church's resources are stretched even farther, we may fall into a struggle to control them. Those of us from the richer countries may seek to use our prosperity as a threat or a club, as a lever to control. And those of us who are financially disadvantaged may, in reaction, fall back among "our own people," resenting the manipulation and seeking a way to assert ourselves against injustice, real or perceived.

The result? Argument, contention, suspicion, name-calling, division. The fragmentation of the church.

The option of block voting. When the voting at a General Conference session divides along national or economic lines, when delegates vote in blocks rather than according to individual conscience, the unity of the church will be imperiled. Then the councils of the church will have degenerated into political gatherings with maneuvering for power and control.

May God deliver us from this option. Already in 1990, at the Indianapolis session that debated the controversial issue of the ordination of women, we saw signs of the council dividing sharply along such lines. This particular question carries so much emotional freight that what happened with regard to it cannot be considered a bellwether for future sessions. But we need to be alert to the possibility. Leaders, in particular, should avoid any attempt to coerce the votes of delegates from their area.

The option of skewed representation. As followers of Jesus, we must stand for nothing less than fairness and equality. This means that a member from a less affluent society has the same vote as one from a stronger part of the world, as well as that Adventists in areas where the work moves slower and numbers remain comparatively small have a voice alongside those where the church is growing fast and has large membership. We must resist the option that would skew representation at the councils of the world church, either giving greater power to "those with the money" or crushing those areas where the work is weak numerically.

The option of national churches. Arguments over race and finances could ultimately lead us to this point. Then we would be like the Lutherans, Methodists, Baptists, and Episcopalians—no longer one world church, but an affiliation of national or regional bodies whose priorities are

85

local rather than global. And the dream of Revelation 14:6, 7 would be shattered.

We must resist this option with every ounce of our beings. Yet we need to realize that the national church idea is less likely to appear as a stand-alone agenda item than as simply the next logical step after yielding to the other options we have outlined above.

I cannot emphasize too strongly the dangers before the church that we have looked at in this chapter. And they are not something for the distant or even near future—they are knocking at the door right now.

What lies ahead? Can we survive the threats of fragmentation that come with our amazing growth worldwide?

Only by the power of the crucified and risen Christ. In Him—and in Him alone—is the answer that no other church, no society has yet found, the power to break down the barriers of race and ethnicity, the power to make and hold together one people from all the world bound up in love, fellowship, doctrine, mission, and hope.

That is my hope for the Seventh-day Adventist Church. *He* is my hope.

And in closing this all too brief treatment of an exceedingly weighty issue, let me mention a couple of positive developments.

First, the church finally is emphasizing financial self-reliance for all divisions. That idea is so elemental that it should have been built into our missionary endeavors from the beginning. But it wasn't and for various reasons, some of which are ugly—for example, control. So long as a field was dependent on funding from abroad, it could be "kept in its place." So some missionaries did not encourage Christian stewardship. I cannot find anything to commend in this approach; it is incredible, part of a colonial attitude that should never have been given a place among us.

Only at the Annual Council held in Bangalore, India, in

1993—yes, *in 1993!*—did the world church take decisive steps to make self-reliance for all fields a reality, not a shibboleth. Incredible that it took us so long, but at last it has come.

Second, in the midst of financial pressures, the Lord has greatly blessed some individual Adventists and put into their hearts a concern for needy projects. In several countries we now have members who have amassed considerable wealth; but not only that—who give generously to fund a variety of initiatives. In terms of the total giving by Adventists, their contributions represent a tiny fraction; but in an era of tight budgets, they have stepped forward to fund evangelistic opportunities, build churches, and so on.

Just one more answer from our wonderful God. With Him are all the answers we need. He *is* the Answer.

CHAPTER
Nine

Many Voices, Many Gurus

T he church in Corinth was fragmenting. Although Christians comprised but a tiny minority from that pagan city, they had split into factions based on leaders of the early church.

Some claimed Peter as their champion. They could point out that he had been personally called into ministry by the Lord Himself and had, with James and John, constituted the inner circle of Jesus' confidants. And wasn't Peter the natural leader among the Twelve and arguably the dominant figure among the fast-growing sect of Christians?

The Apollos party couldn't claim such history for their leader. Apollos was a convert from among the Greeks. But they valued him for qualities in which he outshone Peter. Unlike the fisherman-turned-preacher, who lacked education and finesse, Apollos was a marvelous speaker. He knew the Scriptures inside out and proclaimed Jesus as the Messiah with skill and power that refuted the Jews and confounded the skeptical Greeks.

Paul had a following also. Not that he had tried to build up support for himself—he hadn't, nor had Peter and Apollos. But some of the Corinthians, intent on identifying with a human leader, decided he was their man. And why not? Not only was Paul the apostle par excellence to the Gentile world; he had founded the congregation at Corinth.

Paul had fathered the church, so he, not Peter, Apollos, or anyone else, deserved the right to be chief.

Another faction took the game of one-upmanship even farther. Instead of the Peter party, the Apollos party, or the Paul party, theirs would be the ultimate—the Christ party! Who could beat that? With such a clever choice, they obviously were superior!

When Paul heard about this craziness, he fired off a strong letter. "I appeal to you, brothers, in the name of our Lord Jesus Christ, that all of you agree with one another so that there may be no divisions among you and that you may be perfectly united in mind and thought. My brothers, some from Chloe's household have informed me that there are quarrels among you. What I mean is this: One of you says, 'I follow Paul'; another, 'I follow Apollos'; another, 'I follow Cephas'; still another, 'I follow Christ'" (1 Corinthians 1:10-12).

And, since the Corinthians attached importance to the person who had baptized them instead of to Christ, into whom they had been baptized, he reminded them: "Is Christ divided? Was Paul crucified for you? Were you baptized into the name of Paul? I am thankful that I did not baptize any of you except Crispus and Gaius, so no one can say that you were baptized into my name" (1 Corinthians 1:13, 14).

Dividing their energies, setting up one leader against another, striving to have something to boast about—we can hardly believe the stupidity of those Corinthian Christians. Seventh-day Adventists would never fall into a trap like that—or would we?

Instead of Peter, Apollos, Paul, and Christ, today, we have Venden, Spear, Wieland, and Sequeira. And many more—Knight, Standish, Maxwell, Larson, Waggoner, Jones, Short, Ford, Grosboll, Osborne, and who knows how many others who have been accorded guru status by someone.

The individuals listed above haven't necessarily sought to become Adventist gurus. Most, perhaps all, have resisted this tendency. The problem doesn't lie primarily with them but with Adventists who dote upon their teachings.

"I read everything you write," people will tell you if you are in the publishing business. And if you do a lot of public speaking, they'll want to get audio and video tapes of your messages and send them far and wide to their friends. They will want your autograph and treat you like a celebrity.

All this attention and adulation can flatter you. It can turn your head. Even while murmuring disclaimers, you begin to like the shoes of a guru. But this whole development is unhealthy spiritually—for both teacher/guru and for members/devotees.

We Adventists used to be people of the Book. We used to study for ourselves to "test everything" (1 Thessalonians 5:21). We were careful not to follow slavishly in the teachings of another. We criticized Roman Catholics and other Christians because they permitted a pope, prelate, or preacher to do their thinking for them.

But now we're Corinthianizing. *To Corinthianize* was an actual verb in the ancient world: taking its force from the gross immorality of that city, it meant to throw off all restraint, to go to the dogs in dissolute living. Adventists today give new meaning to the term, as we "Corinthianize" like the early Christians of that city.

Even the religious scholars among us have begun to fragment. Differences of opinion are one thing; institutionalizing differences is far more serious. But that is what is happening.

Consider what happens each fall. Most college and university Bible teachers in North America belong to one or more professional societies—the Society of Biblical

91

Literature, the American Academy of Religion, or the Evangelical Theological Society. These societies convene for an annual meeting that discusses scholarly papers, and the Adventist members—totalling upward of one hundred—typically attend. Because these professional societies usually meet in the same city, Adventist scholars from across North America, and some from abroad, have a chance for fellowship and discussions of particular interest to them.

For nearly twenty years, Adventist scholars have met together in conjunction with these annual conventions. For some time, they met informally, but in the late 1970s they formally organized, elected officers, and chose for themselves the name Andrews Society of Religious Studies (recently changed to the Adventist Society of Religious Studies). By thus constituting themselves they could have their program printed in the official program of the convention, be allotted a meeting room, and so on.

Although this way worked well for several years, fissures began to develop. The gulf grew wider, and this, along with other factors, resulted in the formation of a new society for Adventist scholars—the Adventist Theological Society.

Hence the following scenario, played out in the Washington, D.C., area in 1993 and repeated in other cities each fall. Adventist scholars descended on Washington from the United States, Canada, and several other countries. They joined together in attending the professional meetings, but for the *Adventist* part—the fellowship and "in-house" discussions—they went separate ways. The Adventist Society of Religious Study people met in one location, the Adventist Theological Society folk in another. On Sabbath each group conducted worship services at different area churches.

Although a small number belong to both Adventist

societies, as I write, Adventist scholars as a group remain polarized. I think this is a shameful thing, bad in itself and bad in the message it sends to the young people these scholars are paid to teach.

Each group can present its "case," its arguments. But in light of what our Lord calls us to as His people, are the scholars any better than the Corinthians whom Paul rebuked? I write in sorrow; I gave twenty years of service to Adventist academia and was the first president of the Andrews Society of Religious Studies. Today, I refuse to attend the meeting of either group. Our numbers are too small and the task too great for us to divide our energies in this manner.

Let me make clear that I heartily support open investigation and frank discussion of ideas. This is our Adventist heritage, bequeathed from the earliest days of the movement. We are a people of "present truth" (2 Peter 1:12)—a marvelous concept that invites us to keep on studying and searching, because the Lord will progressively unfold to us new dimensions of truth.

Further, the fact of theological ferment among us in itself is a highly positive thing. It indicates that for us, and in contrast to most other denominations, doctrine still counts for something. We haven't succumbed to a *laissez-faire* attitude to truth, to a lazy ecumenism that robs the Bible of its cutting edge.

Take Martin Weber's recent book, *Who's Got the Truth?* He asked five prominent Adventists—Graham Maxwell, George Knight, Jack Sequeira, Morris Venden, and Ralph Larson to briefly state their understanding of the gospel. Weber then critiqued each statement and dialogued with the author. He closed out the book by elaborating his own position.

The book exposes differences—some major—in the way Adventists understand the gospel. Surely that fact in itself is serious: how can we take "the everlasting gospel" to all the world, as Revelation 14:6, 7 mandates, if we aren't clear on what the message really is?

So what shall we say about a book like this—do we need it or not? Is it better to let the differences come out, or should we keep them under wraps? (A controversial aspect of the book involves Dr. Graham Maxwell. Although he declined the invitation to submit a statement for publication and refused to dialogue with Weber, Weber nonetheless put in his understanding of Maxwell's views and proceeded to critique it. Because of this feature, Adventist publishing houses declined to accept the manuscript; Weber published it privately.)

Leaving aside the flap over the Maxwell material, my view is that the church is helped more than hurt by such exchanges. I have strong confidence in the power of the truth to stand investigation. At the end of the day, after all the facts and arguments have been fully aired, the truth alone will remain.

Many Adventists today are weighing all sorts of theological matters. The issues range from those basic to our message and mission—the nature of inspiration, Creation, the role of Ellen White, what happened in 1888, prophetic interpretation, and, as we saw above, the gospel itself—to the speculative (calculations and surmisings about the date of Jesus' return) to the trivial. Some of us want to make issues out of nonissues, like raising the King James Version to the only biblical version we can trust. Some claim major importance for points of doctrine that as a people we have never made fundamental beliefs—such as the human nature of Christ.

Many voices. Many teachers. Many papers. Many videos.

And overall, the effect is more good than bad, in my judgment.

Good—so long as we search and decide for ourselves.

Good—so long as we don't follow blindly any human leader.

Good—so long as we don't resort to name-calling and labeling those who don't see eye to eye with us.

Good—so long as we realize that we need each other; that "church" means we are all parts of a body, dependent on one another.

Good—so long as we acknowledge that no one has a lock on all truth, that truth is too big to be encompassed by any single human mind, that at best we grasp only aspects of truth filtered through the prism of our individual experience, and that only God, who is Truth, knows and understands truth fully.

Good—so long as we follow the quest for truth through the Holy Spirit, not through a human agency.

Good—so long as we don't turn our teachers into gurus.

Good—so long as we don't Corinthianize.

Only if we can remain on the Good side of all these "so longs" can the church go forward without fragmenting.

Ten

Two Theological Streams

F or some Seventh-day Adventists, 1957 marks a theological turning point. That was the year when *Questions on Doctrine*, the fruitage of extended dialogue between Adventist leaders and evangelicals Donald Barnhouse and Walter Martin, rolled off the presses. Those who criticize the book contend that the Adventists, eager for the denomination to be more widely accepted, gave too much away in these discussions. Particularly, with regard to the human nature of Jesus (the book argues that He took Adam's unfallen nature) and the atonement (*Questions* upholds Calvary as a complete atoning sacrifice).

Questions on Doctrine circulated widely; however, copies are no longer available. Although the book was never repudiated or withdrawn, neither was it reprinted. A negative feature of *Questions* was its anonymous authorship: the group of leaders whose dialogue with Barnhouse and Martin provided the material for the work were never named. Thus, *Questions'* standing was ambiguous, being neither a book voted by official church action nor identified clearly by writers.

Although Adventists today still split over *Questions on Doctrine*, the real divide among us goes back much farther. Not 1957 but 1888 marks the beginning of two distinct theological streams that run side by side within the church to this day.

What we are discussing here goes beyond the doctrinal differences we mentioned in the last chapter. The issues are more fundamental than whether Jesus took Adam's nature before or after the Fall, the 144,000, or some interpretation of prophecy. Further, they probe deeper than the individual differences of understanding in the plan of salvation that we expect to be with us until the Lord comes—we each filter the gospel through our own life history, so inevitably some of us stress one aspect, others a different aspect.

The issues focused on in 1888 at the General Conference session held in Minneapolis, Minnesota, cut to the heart of biblical teaching about Christ's work for us and our response. Christians have wrestled with these issues from the beginning; Adventists first faced them squarely in 1888. We divided over them then, with a struggle that at times was heated; we still are divided, and the struggle continues. So weighty are the issues, so heavy the stakes, that fragmentation is possible. Those independent groups today that seem most likely to form offshoots have this issue at their core.

So much has been written and spoken about 1888, so many differing viewpoints presented, that the average Adventist understandably feels confused. If 1888 is so important, why the debate over what really happened?

The bare facts are available, of course. The session convened in an atmosphere of tension over prophetic interpretation. The point at issue being one we find incredible today—in Daniel's vision of the terrible beast in Daniel 7, were the Huns or the Alamanni one of the horns? Yes, that's what they were arguing about before the session, and that's what they came to argue about! On one side were people like Uriah Smith, who had written extensively on Daniel and Revelation; on the other, the young preachers J. H. Waggoner and A. T. Jones; the *Review and Herald* on the right and the *Signs of the Times* on the left.

But they soon had much more to engage their thinking. At the session Waggoner presented a series of studies on the book of Galatians, in which he argued that "the law" that Paul speaks of as our schoolmaster was not just the ceremonial law but the moral law as well. And that brought the house down.

Outgoing General Conference President George I. Butler couldn't attend the session because of ill health, but he telegrammed the delegates: "Stand by the old landmarks!" Everyone knew what he meant: don't listen to the upstarts Waggoner and Jones. Uriah Smith strongly opposed Waggoner's views, as did "the heavies" almost to a man. Waggoner and Jones were isolated.

But not wholly so. Ellen White took their side, asserting that the Lord was bringing "most precious light" through the two young men. And she found herself isolated. Her messages rejected publicly. It was, she would say later, the most painful chapter in all her long ministry.

These are the bare facts: dispute over the role of the law in salvation, polarization, large-scale rejection of Waggoner's and Jones's emphasis but endorsement of it by Ellen White.

Beyond these facts, the picture becomes murky. Why? Partly because Waggoner's messages at the conference were not recorded. We simply don't know what he said beyond the fact that he included the moral law in the law that is to bring us *to* Christ (but not beyond).

In this vacuum theories proliferate. We know what Waggoner and Jones were preaching and writing *after* 1888, so some claim that's what "the most precious light" was. But Waggoner's and Jones's ideas didn't stay static: they continued to develop, and along lines that eventually became far out. And both messengers, after bitter personal disputes, eventually left the church.

So we are left up in the air after all? No. We don't have Waggoner's sermons from Minneapolis, but we do have Ellen White's messages from the session! We have her prolific writing in the years immediately following, and one emphasis rings loud and clear: righteousness by faith in Jesus alone.

That was her burden in sermon and writing. That was her message in penning the classic *Steps to Christ* in 1892, for which she turned to a non-Adventist publisher, Fleming Revell, to give the glad news widest circulation. That was her theme in *The Desire of Ages* (1898) that soon followed and then in *Christ's Object Lessons* (1900).

Some of the clearest, most compelling statements on the all-sufficiency of Jesus came from her pen during the late 1880s and 1890s. Here are two of my favorites:

> Christ was treated as we deserve, that we might be treated as He deserves. He was condemned for our sins, in which He had no share, that we might be justified by His righteousness, in which we had no share. He suffered the death which was ours, that we might receive the life which was His. "With His stripes we are healed" (*The Desire of Ages*, 25).

> To him who is content to receive without deserving, who feels that he can never recompense such love, who lays all doubts and unbeliefs aside, and comes as a little child to the feet of Jesus, all the treasures of eternal love are a free, everlasting gift (*Manuscript Releases*, 8:186).

Thus, 1888 emerges as a watershed in Adventist history. Here was no totally new understanding of righteousness by faith, something unique in Christian history, but an unambiguous affirmation of Jesus alone as our Saviour.

That emphasis was new to many in 1888. Our pioneers were great preachers and debaters of the law. They could defeat opponents in print and public forums by their knowledge of Scripture; they put the antinomians to rout. On the basis of the Bible itself, they saw their mission as the restorers of the breach in the law as they proclaimed the perpetuity of the seventh-day Sabbath.

God used mightily these men and women who loved Him and gave their all to His cause. But they had much to learn still: in their zeal for the law they had pushed Christ to the side; they had a gospel that added human works to Christ's all-sufficiency.

Now, the gospel always involves the divine side and the human side. Our salvation comes in cooperating with God. Because of this balance of God and humanity, it's easy to distort the gospel, to make it over into a false gospel.

We can, for instance, so play up the divine side that the human is negated. The full development of this thinking leads to the teaching that God determines who will be lost and who will be saved, or alternately, that He will save everyone at last.

On the other hand, we can so stress the human aspect that it becomes primary in the salvation process. Thus, the will emerges as sufficient of itself to obey, or the teaching that says, in effect, that we are dependent on God's grace for our *becoming* a Christian, but after that, we have to work out our own salvation.

Christians have struggled with this balance for many centuries, so it's no wonder that the Minneapolis conference caused such a stir. The specific question there concerned the role of the moral law in salvation, but in essence it was the same old issue.

Unfortunately, the *Review and Herald*, the church's

general paper, played a negative role following the 1888 session. Editor Uriah Smith, who opposed Waggoner and Jones vehemently in Minneapolis, continued his campaign through the pages of the church paper.

In the June 11, 1889, issue of the *Review and Herald*, he wrote an editorial entitled "Our Righteousness."

"The whole object of Christ's work for us is to bring us back to the law," he said, "that its righteousness may be fulfilled in us by our obedience to it, and that when at last we stand beside the law, which is the test of the judgment, we may appear as absolutely in harmony with it. . . . There is then a righteousness that we must have, to be secured by doing and teaching the commandments."

Ellen White penned a stinging response. On June 14 she wrote: "This morning I have read your article in the *Review*." "A noble personage stood beside me and said, 'Uriah Smith . . . is walking like a blind man into the prepared net of the enemy, but he feels no danger because light is becoming darkness to him and darkness light' " (Letter 55, 1889. Published in *The Ellen G. White 1888 Materials* [Washington, D.C.: The Ellen G. White Estate, 1987], 336).

In a sermon given five days later, she urged: "Man must be clothed with Christ's righteousness. Then he can, through the righteousness of Christ, stand acquitted before God . . . .

"Here is our strength, Christ our righteousness. . . . Is that not enough for us?" (Manuscript 5, 1889).

No, it isn't. Our egos, twisted by sin, want to have *some* part, some merit, some credit. That's why God's good news is so easily lost or corrupted.

But the gospel—the good news proclaimed by the Lord— says, With Me you have all you ever need. No need to try to add to what I have done—in fact, you *cannot* add to what

I have done. Be content to receive salvation without deserving it, as a free gift.

The immediate issue that divided the saints in 1888 has passed away. By and large, Adventists accept that Paul includes the moral law in his discussions in Galatians 3. But the issue behind the issue—the balance of the divine and the human—is still very much with us.

Two theological streams flow from Minneapolis. One stream gives priority to the divine, the other to the human. Today, one emphasizes grace, the other victory.

Aren't *both* grace and victory important? Absolutely. The Bible over and over stresses grace alone through faith alone. It also calls us over and over to victorious living in Jesus, reminding us that sin shall not have dominion over us, because we are not under the law but under grace.

But where does the focal point lie—on grace or on victory? On God or on our response to God?

You can take all the Adventist theologians and writers from 1888 to today, and the list falls pretty easily (a few names aren't clear) into one camp or the other. Remember, I am *not* suggesting that those who give priority to grace are soft on sin or that those who emphasize victory are legalistic. In the long list you may find a few who seem indifferent to behavior or who may be legalists, but that's all. The question isn't one *or* the other—grace *or* victory—but rather where shall we put the emphasis?

Having observed the struggle in my own experience as well as in the church, I have firm convictions as to the answer of the Bible and Ellen White's writings. "In the beginning God . . ."—God first, last, and in between, Christ the Alpha and the Omega also. Victory, yes, but not first—grace first, and out of the life overwhelmed with divine favor and overflowing with love and gratitude, then victory.

Grace is extraordinary, totally unlike our experience of the world. We soon learn that in the world we get what we deserve. But grace reverses the human order: the divine order teaches us that we get what we *don't* deserve. God is a profligate Lover and Giver. He welcomes into His kingdom a multitude of unworthy wretches.

You hear a great deal about the gospel, among Adventists and other Christians. But the gospel is always controversial, just as it was in Jesus' day. It especially offends the "good" people, the "pious" who are scrupulous in religious observance, who secretly or not so secretly keep record of their "brownie" points.

The gospel offended the scribes and Pharisees. The gospel offended Smith, Butler, and most of "the brethren" in Minneapolis. The gospel still offends today. Our tendency inevitably is to go the way of the Galatians—to seek to *add on* to the work of Christ.

I believe the Lord is still struggling with the Seventh-day Adventist Church. I believe He has unfinished business from 1888. This struggle accounts for many of the tensions in today's church—and raises the possibility of fragmentation.

The radical independents among us—those who, by appropriating tithe, ordaining clergy, publishing their own literature, and running counter camp meetings, are close to becoming offshoots—all belong on the "human" or "victory" side of the line. (Note that many others on that side do not share their tendencies to fragmenting the church, but are solid, loyal members.) For these radicals, "victory" becomes a key component of a theological package that includes the "sinful" nature of Jesus and the "delay" in the second coming. Christ *had* to be just like us, they assert, so that we can overcome as He overcame, and until God's people reach a state of sinless perfection, He cannot return.

These radicals may combine forces and split away. But

that seems unlikely; they tend to be of such an independent mind-set that the leaders of each faction could not unite under a common head.

Our discussions in this chapter lead me to a final suggestion. Why are so many Adventist churches cold and unwelcoming? Why so little zeal for souls? Why the lack of joy? Why the judgmentalism and criticism? Why the indifference toward strangers and guests?

Perhaps because cold churches and cold Adventists haven't experienced the incredible nature of grace. They haven't yet experienced salvation—indeed, all of life—as a gift.

As a teenager I attended a public school. It was somewhat demanding in its entrance requirements, and once admitted, students soon realized that academics was priority number 1.

For every course, we not only received a grade but a score and our position in that course. All scores were listed: we knew just where we stood in each course in relation to other students, as well as our overall position in the class.

And the seating! The "top" of the class sat in the corner farthest from the teacher, the "dunce" in the middle of the front row!

Yes, I made some good friends in that school, but in spite of, not because of, the system. The system fostered comparison and contrast, feelings of superiority or inferiority, of success or failure.

No grace there. Only works.

No motivation to help another student. Only to get ahead of him.

But when the 1888 message captures the hearts of Seventh-day Adventists, the world will know it. That's because grace liberates us to treat others as God has treated us. And a church liberated from competition, enthralled with the grace of God, will not fragment.

Eleven

A New Church Aborning

A new Seventh-day Adventist Church is emerging—that is the tenth and last reason for the pressures toward fragmentation that we feel all around us. All the factors that we have noticed so far—the spirit of the age, the need for revival, generational differences, the impact of education, frustration over the "delay" in the second coming, the influence of modern technology, ethnic and financial pressures, the many voices and many gurus, and the two theological streams that flow from 1888—converge in this end result. And the prospect of a new church delights some and alarms others.

We feel it in our bones. The church has changed; the church is changing. And we sense that, as Ronald Reagan liked to say, we "ain't seen nothin' yet." Granted that change has always been with us to some extent, that a certain amount is inevitable, the *pace* of change today takes away our breath. Before our eyes, we see it—a new church aborning.

In our next and final chapter, we shall reflect on the dynamics and theology of change. If we already have "the truth," why should there be change? If our organization, structure, financial processes, and way of life have served so well for so many years, why replace them? Aren't we courting disaster? Won't change inevitably weaken the church, dilute its distinctive identity, or cast it on the shoals of ruin?

More on that later; but the question that gnaws at the vitals of long-time Adventists is this: Will I be *comfortable* in the new church? After I have given a lifetime of financial support and diligent effort to build up the church, will it leave me behind? Can I accept the new baby that is coming to birth as mine—or will I call it a bastard?

If time lasts, the Adventist Church of the year A.D. 2000 will differ considerably from the church today, and by the year 2020 it may be so changed that, if a member laid to rest today were to rise from the dead, he or she might hardly recognize it.

For example:

•A church in which Spanish, not English predominates.

•A church in which whites exist as a noticeable but creative minority.

•A church with an Asian General Conference president.

•A church with many women clergy.

•A church with new structures instead of conferences and union conferences.

•A church with a revamped financial organization.

•A church in which the General Conference headquarters functions primarily as a clearinghouse for personnel and ideas and gives spiritual rather than administrative leadership.

All these changes are possible in the new church that is aborning. All, and more. Others that we cannot foresee now.

But rather than try to be futurologists, let us for a moment dream dreams and see visions, as the Lord said people in the last days would do (see Joel 2:28, 29). Let us vision the new church *as it might be*, as it comes to reflect more fully God's will for His people.

Organization and structures are important, but they aren't what church is *really* about. Church is about people—people saved by a loving Lord who treat others as God has treated them, who look not only on their own interests but on the interests of others, who do nothing out of selfish ambition but who have the attitude of Jesus.

So here is my dream for church 2000. Here is my dream for the church that is aborning. What's yours?

Church 2000, first of all, is a body of people who rejoice in salvation by faith. God's grace reigns here; everyone is amazed, stunned, and transformed by the incredible generosity that brought the Son of God down from heaven to live and die in our place on Calvary. Church 2000 wears the robe of Christ's righteousness, and it is pure white, spotless; in it you will find not one thread of human devising.

Church 2000 is also a community of love and acceptance. The men and women and boys and girls who welcome Christ have gained the victory over those prejudices that divide humanity, those prideful distinctions that we absorb from our environment. The power of the gospel has broken down the barriers of racism, casteism, and sexism; these people are one in Christ, fulfilling Jesus' petition in John 17:21-23.

So Church 2000 is a fellowship of equals in which all people are given their rightful place, where equality reigns and the marvelous variety of the human race brings rejoicing rather than preference. In Church 2000, no one lords it over another:

old over young
men over women
whites over blacks
educated over unlearned
rich over poor

Church 2000 shows compassion for the handicapped and the broken.

Church 2000 acts with justice toward all. It is open in its financial affairs, showing honesty and integrity in every transaction.

In Church 2000, leaders are servants of the community, using their office to glorify Christ and to build up His body. They encourage individual expression and participation.

In Church 2000, every talent is utilized, every potential realized, and every resource tapped so that the image of Jesus may be reproduced corporately.

One in hope, one in lifestyle, one in faith, one in shared mission—this is Church 2000.

We have come a long way, but we still have far to go. Often we fall into the "we-they" rut, separating ourselves by our words from the body. "They spent the money . . ." or "The *church* doesn't let us . . . ," we say, as though the church exists apart from us, as if it were concentrated in its leaders or its institutions.

But *we* are the church. *I* am the church. I share and shape the corporate image of the church, share and shape it for good or ill.

And we have been tardy in confronting social norms that contradict the gospel. We were slow to integrate, slow to pay women equal wages for the same work as men, slow to challenge the caste system. In each of these areas, far-sighted legislators were ahead of the church: the church took the path of least resistance, tagging along behind society.

But the ideal community will never be realized if we have to wait on the world. The early Christians did not shrink from bearing the shame and offense of the cross; nor must we. God calls His people to a higher standard, to be different—not only individually but as a body. We must allow His Spirit to roam in our midst, rebuking our pride and prejudice, rooting out differences that deny the gospel, calling us up to the shining mountain.

"And I saw another angel fly in the midst of heaven, having the everlasting gospel to preach unto them that dwell on the earth, and to every nation, and kindred, and tongue, and people, saying with a loud voice, Fear God, and give glory to him; for the hour of his judgment is come: and worship him that made heaven, and earth, and the sea, and the fountains of waters" (Revelation 14:6, 7, KJV). "After this I beheld, and, lo, a great multitude which no man could number, of all nations, and kindreds, and people, and tongues, stood before the throne, and before the Lamb, clothed with white robes, and palms in their hands; and cried with a loud voice, saying, Salvation to our God which sitteth upon the throne, and unto the Lamb" (Revelation 7:9, 10, KJV).

Are you waiting to see the vision turn to reality? So is Jesus: "Christ is waiting with longing desire for the manifestation of Himself in His church. When the character of Christ shall be perfectly reproduced in His people, then He will come to claim them as His own" (*Christ's Object Lessons*, 69).

I have been using A.D. 2000 merely as a reference point, as a date to focus our attention—I do not agree with those who see prophetic significance in that year. We do not know how long our world will continue, although the biblical evidence and the signs all around suggest that time is short.

But "now is the time of God's favor, now is the day of salvation" (2 Corinthians 6:2). As we work to take the good news to all the world, let us also work to make the church— *our church*—the reflection of Christ's character.

111

Will the Church Split?

T he ten factors fragmenting the church that we have looked at in this book—and there are others—could discourage us if we dwelt on them for too long. They indicate that this beloved movement, our church, the Seventh-day Adventist Church, faces daunting challenges in the days immediately ahead.

But I believe the church will meet these challenges and go through intact. I believe it will not split, will not fragment.

Why? For four reasons:

First, because Christ is Head of the church. This is the reason that counts above all others, that gives me most cause for optimism.

"Christ loved the church and gave himself up for her," said the apostle Paul, "to make her holy, cleansing her by the washing with water through the word, and to present her to himself as a radiant church, without stain or wrinkle or any other blemish, but holy and blameless" (Ephesians 5:25-27). Since Christ loved and loves the church so much, the church is safe in His hands.

Now, the headship of Christ does not guarantee that *individually* we can never be lost, because we may choose to spurn His grace; nor can it ensure that *corporately* the Seventh-day Adventist Church cannot fail, because as a people, we may choose to go the way of ancient Israel. We need to heed the warning of their fall from grace.

But what the headship of Christ makes 100 percent certain is: He is able! He is able to best every weapon the evil one raises against the church. He is able to provide wisdom to meet every new situation. He is able to raise up leaders, supply help from unexpected quarters in the most unexpected ways. He is the God of surprises, who has a thousand ways out where we see none, whose mercy and kindness are prodigal in their abundance, whose forgiveness and long-suffering are as boundless as the ocean, as vast as the starry heavens.

The Apocalypse pictures Him as the victorious ruler of the armies of heaven. Can you picture a more vivid scene than this? "I saw heaven standing open and there before me was a white horse, whose rider is called Faithful and True. With justice he judges and makes war. His eyes are like blazing fire, and on his head are many crowns. He has a name written on him that no one but he himself knows. He is dressed in a robe dipped in blood, and his name is the Word of God. The armies of heaven were following him, riding on white horses and dressed in fine linen, white and clean. Out of his mouth comes a sharp sword with which to strike down the nations. 'He will rule them with an iron scepter.' He treads the winepress of the fury of the wrath of God Almighty. On his robe and on his thigh he has this name written: King of Kings and Lord of Lords" (Revelation 19:11-16).

By nature, I am an optimist, but my hope for the church lies outside myself. Jesus, "the head of the body, the church" (Colossians 1:18), the Creator of the universe, the Lamb of Calvary and my Saviour and Lord gives me confidence for the future.

Second, because the Bible foretells only one church at the end of time that follows Jesus and keeps His law.

114

The great vision of Revelation 12 to 14 sketches the history of the church from the birth of Christ to the second coming. Here, we see the struggles of God's people; here, we see the forces of evil arrayed in an end-time confederacy; here we see the last warning messages to be given to planet Earth.

We see also God's people of the last days. They obey the commandments of God and remain faithful to Jesus (Revelation 14:12); they also hold to the testimony of Jesus, which is the Spirit of Prophecy (Revelation 12:17; 19:10).

Although the idea easily leads to spiritual pride, Seventh-day Adventists see themselves in this description. Not that we regard ourselves as better than other Christians or the only people through whom God is working. Rather, we are a prophetic remnant, a creative nucleus around which, we believe, all God's people—now in different communions—will cluster when the lines are drawn clearly just before Jesus returns.

We find no indication in Scripture or the writings of Ellen White that there will be a "remnant of a remnant." Only once did Ellen White even hint that there might need to be another "coming out" due to the divisive spirit that prevailed after the 1888 General Conference session (see *Last Day Events*, 48). Before *and after* that dark experience, she taught just the opposite: the church, weak and defective though it is, remains the object of Christ's supreme regard, and He brings it through the trials of the end time.

Third, because the church has resisted major pressures in the past that seemed about to fragment it.

Roll back the clock ninety years, and try to imagine the state of the church. We are a very small body, only 100,000 or so strong—not even at the mystical 144,000 in membership. Our work and members are concentrated in North America—the world expansion is in its infancy. Battle

Creek, Michigan, symbolizes the church: here we have the General Conference headquarters and the much larger building of the Review and Herald Publishing House.

We have something else in Battle Creek, and it's the pride of the young denomination—the Sanitarium. Adventists may be few in number, but the San is a national and international institution. It is a huge, ornate edifice, and with accommodations for 1,500 patients, it has a staff of 1,800.

Heading the San is the famous, mercurial Dr. John Harvey Kellogg. Renowned surgeon, inventor, speaker, writer, educator, Kellogg is the most public and most powerful Seventh-day Adventist in the world. Although he has an eccentric streak, he is revered as a genius and travels the world to keep the San on the cutting edge of medical practice and health care.

The San would become a mecca for the rich, the famous, and the beautiful. They would flock to it, a "Who's Who" of high society—John D. Rockefeller, Jr., J. C. Penney, Montgomery Ward, George Bernard Shaw, Dale Carnegie, Will Durant, Homer Rodeheaver, Bill Tilden, William Jennings Bryan, Ivan Pavlov, Thomas Edison, Eddie Cantor, Admiral Richard Byrd, Luther Burbank, Booker T. Washington, Billy Sunday, Amelia Earhart, and President William Howard Taft.

Imagine what the loss of the San would mean to Adventists. Imagine the impact if Kellogg split with the church. Could the church survive? Wouldn't it fragment or be weakened beyond healing?

It happened. We lost the San. Kellogg was disfellowshiped after a bitter struggle with General Conference President Arthur Daniels and after repudiating Ellen White.

Adventists packed up and left Battle Creek (the Review and Herald Publishing House had burned to the ground earlier). We made a new beginning in Washington, D.C.

You can see the old picture of the General Conference building in Takoma Park, see it standing so small with open land all around it. Put alongside it a picture of the grand new San that Kellogg built in Battle Creek to replace the old San after it burned, and you'll begin to sense how tough those years must have been for the Seventh-day Adventist Church.

I can think of nothing comparable today. If we lost at a stroke both Loma Linda University and Andrews University, if we saw the defection of a bunch of revered church leaders, that might be getting close. But not very close: today's church is so diverse, so far-flung, that no parallel really holds.

The crisis of ninety years ago wasn't the only one we've faced, although it surely was the greatest in our history.

Financial pressures? That's the way we began. We've never had enough money for all that we wanted to do. But the Lord has provided, taught us to prioritize, and driven us to our knees over and over again.

Theological splits? They've come along every thirty or forty years. But they've never led to a breakup of the church: the offshoots shoot off, sometimes with a big noise, but fizzle out.

Leaders who defect? Plenty of them, in the nineteenth and through the twentieth centuries. Stars that impress us with their brilliance plunge into darkness—through immorality or strange doctrinal ideas or discouragement or the pull of the world. But the work goes on; the church continues.

"The church may appear as about to fall, but it does not fall," wrote Ellen White in 1886 (*Selected Messages*, 2:380). That was just before a theological crisis that came to a head in 1888. And that has been the story of this church from the beginning.

I think it's a wonderful story. A story of God's long-suffering and grace. Of His providence. Of His guiding, protecting hand.

Fourth, because John saw the church of the last days, and saw it victorious.

Here they are: Then I looked, and there before me was the Lamb, standing on Mount Zion, and with him 144,000 who had his name and his Father's name written on their foreheads. And I heard a sound from heaven like the roar of rushing waters and like a loud peal of thunder. The sound I heard was like that of harpists playing their harps. And they sang a new song before the throne and before the four living creatures and the elders. No one could learn the song except the 144,000 who had been redeemed from the earth. These are those who did not defile themselves with women, for they kept themselves pure. They follow the Lamb wherever he goes. They were purchased from among men and offered as firstfruits to God and the Lamb. No lie was found in their mouths; they are blameless" (Revelation 14:1-5).

And in case that number 144,000 throws you off kilter, study this scene that John also saw.

After this I looked and there before me was a great multitude that no one could count, from every nation, tribe, people and language, standing before the throne and in front of the Lamb. They were wearing white robes and were holding palm branches in their hands. And they cried out in a loud voice: "Salvation belongs to our God, who sits on the throne, and to the Lamb." . . . Then one of the elders asked me, "These in white robes—who are they, and where did they come from?" I answered, "Sir, you know." And he

said, "These are they who have come out of the great
tribulation; they have washed their robes and made
them white in the blood of the Lamb. Therefore,
they are before the throne of God
and serve him day and night in his
temple;
and he who sits on the throne will spread
his tent over them.
Never again will they hunger;
never again will they thirst.
The sun will not beat upon them,
nor any scorching heat.
For the Lamb at the center of the throne
will be their shepherd;
he will lead them to springs of living
water.
And God will wipe away every tear from
their eyes" (Revelation 7:9, 10, 13-17).

So God *will* have a people who love Him supremely in the
last days. To them He will be more precious than any
human or any earthly possession. Because they have been
overwhelmed by His grace, they are ready to go to the
death, if necessary, for Him.

What Can We Do?

I believe that God wants to enlist our cooperation in His
purposes. Christ is Lord and Head of the church, yes; but
He wants us to work with Him. He wants us to be intelligent, thoughtful men and women who are filled with the
Holy Spirit and alert to the needs of the times.

We have a part to play in helping prevent the fragmentation of the church. I think of at least three areas where
leaders, especially, but also every member who cares
enough can make a difference.

First, by helping our people cope with change. We need a theology of change, a biblical view of change.

Change isn't bad per se. We are creationists—our God created and is the Creator. He brings the light out of darkness, the new out of the old. Every springtime teaches that lesson.

Only that which is dead doesn't change. Change is built into the fabric of the universe.

Change forces itself upon the church from three perspectives:

1. Growth brings change. A baby doesn't stay a baby—it grows, and as it grows, it changes. It remains in continuity with the past, but it is transformed. It's the same person but scarcely recognizable.

God wants the church to grow. And how it has grown and is growing! Let's not be surprised that its growth brings changes.

2. Changing times demand a changing church. Shouldn't the church be "the pillar and foundation of the truth" (1 Timothy 3:15)? Absolutely. But not everything is bad in the world; not every change is of the devil.

Do we want to become like the Amish? They attempted to freeze the church in time. Whatever witness they bear—and I'm sure they are sincere people—is severely limited by their withdrawal from society.

And, let's not forget, their attempt to resist change and preserve "purity" hasn't worked. So we find them arguing—and splitting!—over whether they should have black or chrome bumpers on their horse buggies! All this while people commit suicide, babies starve, and multitudes go down into Christless graves.

3. God wants to change us into His image. That means individually and collectively. It means doctrinally as well as spiritually. It means that He wants us to keep on the leading edge of His will, to remain a people of "present

truth," because He has a lot of good things for us to learn and understand and some things to unlearn.

And because we believe in the Holy Spirit, the doctrine of the Spirit is right there in our twenty-seven Fundamental Beliefs. But the Spirit guides us into all truth (see John 16:13); the Spirit brings life and freedom.

That means change—of God's ordering.

So let's not be afraid of change. Let's not advocate change willy-nilly—change merely for the sake of change—but let's encourage change as the Bible teaches, and indeed, demands.

Second, by clarifying what it means to be a Seventh-day Adventist.

You can find enormous differences among us as to the essence of Adventism—all the way from salvation by gluten to calculating the year of the Lord's return.

We need to think globally—on a world scale—as to what this church is all about. Let's work at a *minimum*, not a maximum, list. That way we can zero in on what matters most and know where we need to throw up the bulwarks as we seek to cooperate with the Lord in preserving the miracle of the Seventh-day Adventist Church.

The twenty-seven Fundamentals are an important start. If we lose our doctrinal unity, we'll likely lose everything. But how well do the twenty-seven play around the world? How much do their good words mean to people without education, from vastly different backgrounds? Do we need a simplified version? And are there areas of theology that we, from the developed countries, may be overlooking? Has the time come for the *world* church to impact our theology in a significant way?

Questions, not answers. I don't have the answers. I strongly recommend that as a people we address these questions.

We're a people of hope—that is basic, so the second

coming must always be central.

We're a people of the Sabbath—so the law must ever be prominent but placed in a grace orientation.

And we're a people of the Bible.

And a people with the gift of prophecy.

And the message of the sanctuary.

And we have a mission to the world.

And God calls us to *live* as His children, to represent Him in these last days.

Keep it short. Keep it basic. Keep it global. But let's get it down, so far as we can: what *really* counts for our worldwide unity. Then let's direct our efforts to holding that fort.

Finally, by educating members on the implications of the gospel.

We haven't done very well in the past. We've seemed to assume that conversion will take care of problems of racism and sexism, that the waters of baptism will wash away pride and prejudice.

So the record leaves a lot to be desired. In North America, a white church and a black church. In Africa, tribalism. In India, casteism.

And when Rwanda erupted in bitter intertribal bloodshed in 1994, where were the Adventists? With our three hundred thousand members, some 16 percent of the population, how much difference did we make? Were Adventists a model of how Hutus and Tutsis could overcome suspicion and hatred, could resist the extreme pressures of tribalism? The answer cuts me to the core—No.

We *have* to take the lessons of Rwanda and the lessons of our past to heart. We *have* to educate our people in what it means to be one in Christ Jesus.

We have delayed far too long. It's time to cease taking the easy road, going along with social structures that pander to tribe and caste. It's time to bite the bullet. It's

time to teach Adventists—all, pastors and members—
what the gospel means in interpersonal relationships.

I'm glad to have a part, to have the privilege of cooperating with the Lord in building up His church. To me, this
is a marvelous privilege. I want to be part of the solution,
not the problem. I want to help preserve the miracle.

Do you?

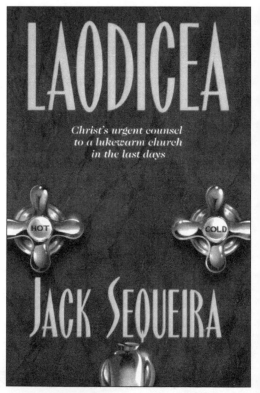

MONUMENT
OR
MOVEMENT?

To what extent is God dependent upon Adventism for "finishing the work"? Is more and bigger always better? What dangers are built into the very heart of Adventism's success? How does reliance upon tradition affect our ability to think biblically?

These are some of the hard questions tackled by George R. Knight in *The Fat Lady and the Kingdom.* Knight looks at church structure, policies, and institutions and questions Adventism's ability to accomplish its mission. A courageous new book that calls us to honesty, accountability, and getting the advent movement moving again. Paper. US$11.95/Cdn$17.35.

THE **FAT LADY AND THE KINGDOM**

Confronting the challenges of change and secularization

Has the church become too ponderous to fulfill its mission?

GEORGE R. KNIGHT

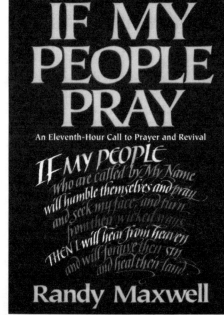

A revival is coming. Will you be a part of it?

What would happen in our homes, churches, and communities if we followed God's counsel in 2 Chronicles 7:14, humbled ourselves, and prayed? That question is explored and answered in Randy Maxwell's *If My People Pray*, a book infused with a passion for prayer as God's chosen method for establishing His kingdom through us and supplying our greatest needs.

If you've had it with status quo Christianity and thirst for a genuine prayer experience that results in revival, get this book and begin praying today. Paper, 192 pages. US$10.95/Cdn$15.90.

Available at your local Adventist Book Center, or call toll free 1-800-765-6955.

Conquering the Dragon Within
by Marvin Moore

As the end draws near, Satan—the dragon—attacks Christians with overpowering temptations and enslaving addictions and taunts us with our failures. Can we defeat him?

Marvin Moore, author of *The Crisis of the End Time*, and editor

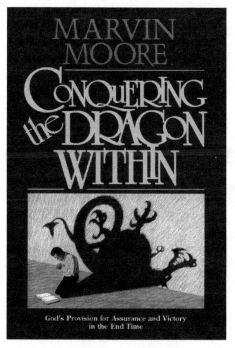

of *Signs of the Times*, uses the counsel of Scripture, Spirit of Prophecy, and the Twelve-Step recovery program to show that through Christ, character change and victory over sin are certain. This intensely practical book provides hands-on devotional exercises for biblical reflection and study at the end of each chapter. Must reading for those wanting God's assurance and victory in the end times.

Hardcover.

US$13.95/Cdn$20.25.

Available at your local ABC or call toll free 1-800-765-6955.

Books You Just Can't Put Down
from PACIFIC PRESS